I0438732

Minimum Pool and Bull Trout Prey Base Investigations at Beulah Reservoir—Final Report for 2008

By Brien P. Rose and Matthew G. Mesa

Prepared in cooperation with the Bureau of Reclamation

Open-File Report 2009–1068

U.S. Department of the Interior
U.S. Geological Survey

U.S. Department of the Interior
KEN SALAZAR, Secretary

U.S. Geological Survey
Suzette M. Kimball, Acting Director

U.S. Geological Survey, Reston, Virginia: 2009

For more information on the USGS—the Federal source for science about the Earth, its natural and living resources, natural hazards, and the environment, visit http://www.usgs.gov or call 1-888-ASK-USGS.
For an overview of USGS information products, including maps, imagery, and publications, visit *http://www.usgs.gov/pubprod*

To order this and other USGS information products, visit *http://store.usgs.gov*

Suggested citation:
Rose, B.P., and Mesa, M.G., 2009, Minimum pool and bull trout prey base investigations at Beulah Reservoir—Final report 2008: U.S. Geological Survey Open-File Report 2009–1068, 54 p.

Any use of trade, product, or firm names is for descriptive purposes only and does not imply endorsement by the U.S. Government.

Although this report is in the public domain, permission must be secured from the individual copyright owners to reproduce any copyrighted material contained within this report.

Contents

Figures

Figures—Continued

Tables

Conversion Factors, Datums, and Acronyms

SI to Inch/Pound

Multiply	By	To obtain
Length		
centimeter (cm)	0.3937	inch (in.)
millimeter (mm)	0.03937	inch (in.)
meter (m)	3.281	foot (ft)
kilometer (km)	0.6214	mile (mi)
Area		
square meter (m^2)	0.0002471	acre
Volume		
liter (L)	0.2642	gallon (gal)
cubic kilometer (km^3)	0.2399	cubic mile (mi^3)
Mass		
gram (g)	0.03527	ounce, avoirdupois (oz)
kilogram (kg)	2.205	pound avoirdupois (lb)
Energy		
joule (J)	0.0000002	kilowatthour (kWh)

Temperature in degrees Celsius (°C) may be converted to degrees Fahrenheit (°F) as follows:
$$°F=(1.8×°C)+32.$$
Temperature in degrees Fahrenheit (°F) may be converted to degrees Celsius (°C) as follows:
$$°C=(°F-32)/1.8.$$

Concentrations of chemical constituents in water are given either in milligrams per liter (mg/L) or micrograms per liter (µg/L).

Acronyms

FWS	United States Fish and Wildlife Service
NFMR	North Fork Malheur River
RBT	rainbow trout
DO	dissolved oxygen
FL	fork length
CPUE	catch per unit effort
h	hour
FPH	fish per hour

Minimum Pool and Bull Trout Prey Base Investigations at Beulah Reservoir—Final Report for 2008

By Brien P. Rose and Matthew G. Mesa

Abstract

Beulah Reservoir in southeastern Oregon provides irrigation water to nearby farms and supports an adfluvial population of threatened bull trout (*Salvelinus confluentus*). Summer drawdowns in the reservoir could affect forage fish production and overwintering bull trout. To assess the impacts of drawdown, we sampled fish, invertebrates, and water-quality variables seasonally during 2006–08. In 2006, the summer drawdown was about 68 percent of full pool, which was less than a typical drawdown of 85 percent. We detected few changes in pelagic invertebrate densities, and catch rates, abundance, and sizes of fish when comparing values from spring to values from fall. We did note that densities of benthic insects in areas that were dewatered annually were lower than those from areas that were not dewatered annually. In 2007, the drawdown was 100 percent (to run-of-river level) and resulted in decreases in abundance of invertebrates as much as 96 percent, decreases in catch rates of fish as much as 80 percent, decreases in abundance of redside shiners (*Richardsonius balteatus*) and northern pikeminnow (*Ptychocheilus oregonensis*) as much as 93 percent, and decreased numbers of small fish in catches. In the fall 2007, we estimated the total biomass of forage fish to be 76 kilograms, or about one-quarter of total biomass of forage fish in 2006. Bioenergetics modeling suggested that ample forage for about 1,000 bull trout would exist after a moderate drawdown, but that forage remaining after a complete dewatering would not be sufficient for a population one-fifth the size. Our results indicate that drawdowns in Beulah Reservoir affect the aquatic community and perhaps the health and well-being of bull trout. The severity of effects depends on the extent of drawdown, population size of bull trout, and perhaps other factors.

Introduction

Bull trout (*Salvelinus confluentus*) were listed by the U. S. Fish and Wildlife Service (FWS) as a threatened species under the Endangered Species Act in 1998. Populations of bull trout are decreasing throughout their range and the State of Oregon has listed the North Fork Malheur River (NFMR) population as one "of special concern." As a result, managers have spent considerable time and effort identifying, restoring, and preserving critical habitat and various life history forms (Muhlfeld and others, 2003). Reasons for the decrease of bull trout in the Malheur River basin include habitat degradation and fragmentation, losses through unscreened diversions, historic chemical treatment projects (Ratliff and Howell, 1992), and entrainment through Agency Valley Dam on the NFMR.

Beulah Reservoir, which was formed after Agency Valley Dam was completed in 1935, currently supports a lacustrine-adfluvial population of bull trout that over-winter in the reservoir from November through early May (Gonzalez, 1998; Schwabe and Tiley, 1999). Over-wintering behavior of bull trout is similar in Flathead Lake, Montana, and Lake Billy Chinook, Oregon (Fraley and Shepard, 1989; Beauchamp and Van Tassell, 2001). Because the reservoir provides irrigation water to nearby farms and ranches, bull trout can experience changes in water level, habitat, and forage availability due to seasonal reservoir drawdowns. Furthermore, reservoir volume occasionally decreases to run-of-river levels, which could severely affect forage fish populations. Decreased forage fish populations could negatively affect the bull trout population in the NFMR drainage by contributing to decreased growth and survival.

Understanding the resilience of the aquatic community in Beulah Reservoir to drawdown and occasional dewatering is important for assessing the effects of reservoir operations on bull trout. Open systems like streams and rivers generally are considered resilient to disturbances such as severe drought (Bayley and Osborne, 1993) and flooding (Matthews, 1986). Such resilience probably is due to large numbers of individuals in nearby tributaries or reaches that can quickly re-colonize disturbed areas (Mathews, 1986; Bayley and Osborne, 1993). In contrast, reservoir fish communities may be more confined and less resilient to environmental disturbance. Drastic or ill-timed changes in the water level of reservoirs can lead to the dewatering of spawning habitat, eggs, and larval fishes (Lantz and others, 1967; Estes, 1972), reduced growth and survival of fishes (Graham and others, 1981), and changes in aquatic vegetation, water chemistry, primary production, and the benthic food web (Benson and Hudson, 1975; Nichols, 1975; Woods and Falter, 1982; Gaboury and Patalas, 1984; Furey and others, 2006). Information on the resilience of the aquatic community in Beulah Reservoir to water-level changes would be useful for the management of threatened bull trout.

The FWS and the Bureau of Reclamation recently completed a Biological Opinion that addresses terms and conditions to minimize the effects of operations at Beulah Reservoir on bull trout. These terms (along with others) establish the need for conservation pool requirements based on water year conditions that supply adequate habitat and forage for bull trout in the reservoir. To assist in this endeavor, we (1) documented species composition, abundance, and distribution of forage fish in Beulah Reservoir in early spring and late fall, before and after summer drawdown; (2) described seasonal variation in aquatic insect abundance and distribution; (3) conducted bioenergetics modeling exercises to evaluate the consumption and growth of bull trout under varying levels of prey availability; and (4) evaluated previous data for Beulah Reservoir that might provide additional information on current conditions. We used this information to evaluate the effects of typical seasonal drawdowns and complete dewatering of the reservoir on various metrics of the aquatic community.

Study Site.—Agency Valley Dam was built by the Bureau of Reclamation on the NFMR during 1934–35 at river km (rkm) 29 and formed Beulah Reservoir (fig. 1). The impoundment provides irrigation water to local farms and some flood control and has no facilities for upstream or downstream passage of fish. The reservoir is 1,020 m above sea level at full pool and has an average width of 1.9 km and a length of about 4 km. The NFMR and Warm Springs Creek enter from the north and the NFMR exits from the south end of the reservoir. The north end of the reservoir is relatively shallow (<10 m deep) with a low gradient bottom. The south end of the reservoir has a steep decline from shore and reaches a maximum depth of about 23 m. Although summer temperatures exceed 20°C at all depths throughout the reservoir (Petersen and others, 2003), it cools rapidly in the fall and typically ices over in winter. Beulah Reservoir is eutrophic (Bureau of Reclamation, 2002) with high abundances and diverse size classes of redside shiners (*Richardsonius balteatus*), redband trout (*Oncorhynchus mykiss gairdneri*), suckers (*Catostomus* sp.), and northern pikeminnow (*Ptychocheilus oregonensis*) (Petersen and others, 2003). The reservoir is stocked with hatchery rainbow trout (RBT) each spring.

Methods

Water-Quality Sampling

We collected data on water quality (and sampled fish and aquatic insects) in Beulah Reservoir during spring (late March through early June) and fall (October through mid-November) of 2006 and 2007, and in only spring 2008. Water temperature, dissolved oxygen (DO), and water transparency were measured about every 2 weeks in three areas of the reservoir: (1) the deep, southern end; (2) the moderately deep, middle of the reservoir (when water depths were sufficient); and (3) the shallow northern end. Water temperature (°C) and DO (mg/L) were measured every meter from the surface to the bottom with a Yellow Springs Instruments© Model 85 multimeter. Reservoir transparency was determined with a Secchi disk. Reservoir volume, river flows, and river temperature data were obtained from Bureau of Reclamation gaging stations (www.usbr.gov/pn/hydromet, accessed February 27, 2009).

Aquatic Insect Sampling

We estimated the density and biomass of pelagic insects in the reservoir using a 0.5-m², 500-µm mesh conical zooplankton net towed vertically from about 1-m above the bottom to the water surface. During spring and fall, we conducted three net tows from randomly selected sites within each of four geographic areas (that is, northwest, northeast, southwest, and southeast) of the reservoir and combined catches into four composite samples by area. The samples were preserved in the field with 70 percent ethanol. In the laboratory, organisms were identified to Order and number and total weight recorded (blotted dry and adjusted to approximate living weights; Howmiller, 1972). Mean weights of individuals were calculated by dividing the total number of insects per sample by their combined weight. Samples were averaged to derive metrics for the reservoir in each season.

We also estimated the abundance and biomass of benthic insects in substrates that experienced different levels of dewatering. We used data from 1977 to 2005 on reservoir elevations after summer drawdown (www.usbr.gov/pn/hydromet, accessed February 27, 2009) to estimate areas of reservoir substrates that were frequently, occasionally, or usually not dewatered. Substrates that were frequently dewatered were higher than 1,010-m elevation and represented about 25 percent of reservoir depths; substrates that were occasionally dewatered ranged from 997- to 1,010-m elevation and represented about 62 percent of reservoir depths; and the typically inundated substrates were less than 997-m elevation and represented about 13 percent of reservoir depths. We collected two benthic samples from random locations within these strata using a Ponar© dredge during the spring when the reservoir was nearly full. We repeated this process every 2 weeks and processed samples as described above.

Fish Sampling

Fish were sampled about every other week with experimental gillnets and fyke nets. The gillnets were 36.5 m long by 3.0 m deep and contained six 6-m panels with stretch mesh sizes of 8.9, 7.6, 6.3, 5.1, 3.8, and 2.5 cm. Gillnets generally were fished on the bottom during daylight hours for 30 min or less. Fyke nets (91 cm height, 122 cm width, and 0.6-cm mesh size) were set with a 13-m center lead extending to shore and fished overnight. We used a stratified (that is, by general geographic region—northwest, northeast, southwest, and southeast) randomized design to establish sampling locations for each gear type with sample sites replaced at the start of each session. Captured fish were anesthetized (using either 50 mg/L Finquel® MS-222 for non-game fish and bull trout or one tablet of Alka-Seltzer Gold© in 2.5 L of water for game fish), identified to species (except for sculpins), measured for fork length (FL, in mm), weighed (only a subsample to the nearest 0.1 g), marked (by removing a fin or placing a Floy© tag in the dorsal musculature for fish >150 mm), and released. Later, we estimated the weights of individuals that were not weighed using the length-weight relation derived from fish that we did weigh.

We estimated the population abundance for the most common fish (including young-of-year, subadult, and adult fish) in the spring and fall using the Schumacher-Eschmeyer estimator for multiple census mark-recapture studies (Schneider, 1998). We assumed compliance with all assumptions associated with this estimator (see Lagler, 1956, for a summary). During spring, we ended population estimates of RBT before the release of hatchery fish into the reservoir. Population estimates during fall, however, included all RBT that were <156 mm. We derived biomass estimates for each species by multiplying the mean weight of fish in each cohort by their estimated population size.

Insect and Fish Response to Reservoir Drawdown

To examine the effects of reservoir drawdown on aquatic insects and fish in Beulah Reservoir, we compared several metrics between seasons (and years) from our sampling. For our pelagic insect data, we compared mean density of insects collected during each season and year. Because few planktonic chironomids were captured during fall, we restricted their analysis to spring data only. We derived the same metrics for benthic chironomids and compared values for those collected from areas that were frequently, occasionally, or generally not dewatered using data from 2006 and 2007 combined and for each sample year using pooled data from the three categories of benthic strata. We also compared the mean mass of benthic chironomids from each reservoir strata. All statistical comparisons of invertebrate data were done with a Kruskal-Wallis test (α =0.05) followed by the Dunn-Šidák post-test procedure to maintain a tolerable experimentwise α level (Sokal and Rohlf, 2003).

We compared the mean fyke net and gillnet catch rates (CPUE) of dace, northern pikeminnow, redside shiner, suckers, and white crappie by number and biomass between consecutive seasons (for example, spring versus fall 2006, fall 2006 versus spring 2007, and so on) with analysis of variance (ANOVA) followed by the Bonferroni post-test procedure (Sokal and Rohlf, 2003). All catch data were $\log_{10}(x+1)$ transformed prior to analysis but are presented untransformed here. Standardized length frequency distributions (by N per 24 h) of fish captured in fyke and gillnets were plotted for the more common fish species (northern pikeminnow, suckers, and redside shiners) by season. We excluded RBT from statistical comparisons because we could not determine the influence that stocked fish had on our results. We also qualitatively compared the Fulton condition factor (Nielsen and Johnson, 1983) of bull trout for different periods and to fish from other areas.

Bioenergetics Modeling

We used a bioenergetics model parameterized for lake trout (*Salvenlinus namaycush*; Stewart and others, 1983) to estimate the seasonal food consumption of bull trout in Beulah Reservoir. The lake trout model has been used in previous work with bull trout (Beauchamp and Van Tassell, 2001), and because these two species are closely related and occupy similar ecological niches, the parameters of the lake trout model are reasonable surrogates for those of bull trout.

The intent of our simulations was to determine if sufficient prey exists in Beulah Reservoir after summer drawdown to sustain a population of bull trout of a certain size from fall through spring. Consumption was estimated for two *hypothetical* populations: (1) the mean estimated spawning population of bull trout in the NFMR (N = 188; Schwabe and others, 2006); and (2) a population of 1,000 adult bull trout, which is an abundance recovery criterion for isolated populations of these fish (Malheur Watershed Council and Burns Piute Tribe, 2004). We ran simulations from November 1 to May 29 (210 days) using three hypothetical growth rates: (1) low—0.01 g per day, which represented a maintenance growth rate of 1 percent; (2) medium—0.64 g per day, which was estimated from bull trout in the NFMR (Schwabe and Tiley, 1999; B Rose and M Mesa, USGS, unpub. data, 2008); and (3) high—2.3 g per day, which was estimated from bull trout in Lake Billy Chinook, Oregon (Beauchamp and Van Tassell, 2001). The initial biomass of fish on day 1 (about 231 g) was derived by subtracting the observed growth rate of bull trout in the NFMR from the mean mass of bull trout collected in the spring from Beulah Reservoir (Schwabe and Tiley, 1999; this report). Final biomass of bull trout (on day 210) was dependent on the growth scenario used in the simulation. As such, simulations using the medium growth rate approximated the mean size of bull trout that overwinter in the reservoir. We obtained temperature data for the simulations from the literature (Bureau of Reclamation, 2002; Petersen and Kofoot, 2002; Peterson and others, 2003; Rose and Mesa, 2007) and from our fieldwork (table 1). We assumed that bull trout would feed in reservoir areas with temperatures near their maximum feeding temperature (see Mesa and others, 2007) and that they would not occupy the reservoir from late spring to fall because of high temperatures.

To provide input on diet composition to the model, we analyzed stomach contents from 10 bull trout (range of FL = 263–286 mm) captured in Beulah Reservoir during spring and fall 2007. These fish ate a variety of organisms (table 2) and we used the mean proportions by weight of invertebrates and fish from the stomach samples as input to the model. For some of our simulations, we assumed that bull trout ate only fish during the fall (simulation days 1-30) and had a diet comprised of 60 percent fish, 20 percent insects, and 20 percent zooplankton in the spring (days 121–210). The model interpolated the diet of bull trout for simulation days 31–120. Mass of zooplankton eaten by bull trout was estimated using the length-weight relation for *Daphnia* (Pechen, 1965) assuming a mean length of 2.5 mm (Wilhelm and others, 1999). The mass of preserved Dipterans was adjusted to approximate living mass (Howmiller, 1972). We also conducted simulations using a diet comprised of only fish and assumed an indigestible fraction of 3 and 15 percent of total biomass for fish and invertebrates (Beauchamp and Van Tassell, 2001). The energy density of common prey fish in Beulah Reservoir ($N = 9$–10 for each species) was measured with bomb calorimetry during spring and fall 2006 and used as input to the model. Overall, energy density of prey fish ranged from 5.07 to 5.63 kJ/g (table 3). Energy densities for prey items used in our model simulations were 5.35 kJ/g (days 1–30) and 5.37 kJ/g (days 121–210) for fish, 3.35 kJ/g for chironomids, and 3.56 kJ/g for zooplankton (Luecke and Brandt, 1993; Beauchamp and others, 1995).

Our fieldwork provided estimates of the abundance and biomass of prey fish available for bull trout in Beulah Reservoir during falls 2006 and 2007. We ran separate simulations for each year assuming a prey fish abundance of about 122,000 and a biomass of 266 kg in fall 2006 and about 23,000 and 76 kg in fall 2007. These numbers reflect the extent of reservoir drawdown in each year, with 2006 being moderately dewatered and 2007 being completely dewatered. Because bull trout can feed on fish as much as 50 percent of their length (Beauchamp and Van Tassell, 2001); all fish <156 mm (mean bull trout length × 0.5) were considered vulnerable to predation by bull trout. For our analysis, we plotted the decrease in prey biomass during the simulation period for each set of assumptions (that is, population size, growth rates, and diet composition) to determine if prey biomass could limit the production of bull trout.

Results

Reservoir Volume and Streamflow

The volume of Beulah Reservoir and flow from the NFMR varied greatly during the study (fig. 2). In spring 2006, Beulah Reservoir was filled to 99 percent of its 0.07 km^3 (59,900 acre-ft) capacity and was drawn down from early summer through fall to 0.023 km^3 (18,656 acre-ft). This represented a drawdown of about 68 percent, which was less than the mean drawdown of 85 percent from 1977 to 2005. Mean ($\pm$ SD) daily streamflow in the NFMR upstream of Beulah Reservoir was 7.0 $\pm$ 8.9 m^3/s, which was about twice the 10-year (1998–2007) average of 3.6 $\pm$ 3.7 m^3/s. In 2007, Beulah Reservoir filled to 84 percent of its capacity and was drawn down to run-of-river level on August 30. During this dewatering, most of the reservoir was shallow (<0.2 m) and maximum depths were about 1 m. Except for several suckers, large numbers of fish mortalities upstream of the dam were not evident. Downstream of the dam, however, a large fish kill did occur (fig. 3). Mean flow in the NFMR was 2.0 $\pm$ 1.4 m^3/s, or about 55 percent of average. During spring 2008, Beulah Reservoir was filled to 89 percent of capacity, and, as of July 30, mean flow in the NFMR was 3.9 $\pm$ 3.7 m^3/s, or about 65 percent of the 10-year average.

Water Quality

Mean daily water temperatures at the outflow of Beulah Reservoir ranged from near 0 in winter to greater than 20°C in summer depending on the year (fig. 4). There was substantial variation in temperatures during early spring 2008 and spring and summer temperatures in 2007 were warmer than temperatures in 2006 and 2008. Reservoir temperature and DO profiles were similar for each sampling site. Temperatures near the bottom of the reservoir were less than 13° C for all sample sites and study periods (fig. 5). Dissolved-oxygen concentrations were less than 6.5 mg/L throughout most of the reservoir only on October 14, 2006 (fig. 6). Stratification occurred during spring 2006 and again during early May 2008, but anoxic conditions near the bottom did not develop. Water clarity varied among study periods and years (fig. 7). In all years, Secchi depths generally were lower in the fall than in the spring. In the spring, Secchi depths were lowest in 2006 (mean $\pm$ SD; 1.2 $\pm$ 0.3 m), highest in 2008 (2.5 $\pm$ 0.3 m), and intermediate in 2007 (2.0 $\pm$ 0.3 m). In the fall, Secchi depths were higher in 2006 (1.1 $\pm$ 0.2 m) than in 2007 (0.7 $\pm$ 0.4 m).

Pelagic Invertebrates

Pelagic invertebrates representing seven Orders were collected from 2006 to 2008. The most common were Hydracarina and Diptera (primarily chironomids). Others collected (in descending order of abundance) included Ephemeroptera, Odonata, Coleoptera, Trichoptera, and Oligochaeta. Mean Hydracarina densities ranged from 0 during fall 2007 to 1.55 $\pm$ 1.21 individuals/m^3 during spring 2007 (fig. 8). Mean densities of Hydracarina in the spring 2007 were significantly higher than mean densities in falls 2006 and 2007 ($P < 0.01$). No other comparisons were statistically significant.

Chironomid densities were highest during spring 2006 (0.57 ± 0.67 individuals/m^3), lowest during spring 2008 (none captured), and intermediate during spring 2007 (0.15 ± 0.18 individuals/m^3; fig. 8). Only two chironomids were captured during falls 2006 and 2007. Differences, however, in the springtime densities of chironomids between the years were not significant.

Benthic Invertebrates

Benthic invertebrates representing three Orders were collected during our study, including Dipterans (primarily chironomids), Oligochaetes, and Trichopterans (in descending order of abundance). For all years combined, the mean densities of Dipterans (by number and biomass) were significantly ($P < 0.01$) lower in areas of the reservoir that were frequently dewatered (100 ± 190 individuals/m^3 and 0.7 ± 0.7 g/m^3) when compared to areas that were occasionally dewatered (785 ± 426 individuals/m^3 and 26.8 ± 11.1 g/m^3) and usually not dewatered ($1,311 \pm 834$ individuals/m^3 and 51.8 ± 36.1 g/m^3; fig. 9). Dipterans collected from areas that were frequently dewatered also were significantly ($P < 0.01$) smaller (0.01 ± 0.01 g) than dipterans collected from other areas (0.04 ± 0.01 g). Overall, the mean densities of benthic dipterans in the spring were significantly lower in 2008 than in 2006 and 2007 (fig. 10). Compared to 2006 and 2007, the densities of benthic chironomids in the spring decreased from 84 to 96 percent in 2008.

Fish Sampling Overview

We sampled with both gear types throughout the reservoir (figs. 11 and 12) and the effort was relatively similar between spring and fall of each year. In total, we captured 33,175 fish in 8,678 h of sampling with small mesh fyke nets and gillnets (table 4). Fish captured in fyke nets comprised 98 percent of our total catch. The most common fish species by number were redside shiners (54 percent of total catch) and northern pikeminnow (32 percent of total catch). In contrast, RBT and largescale suckers (*Catostomus macrocheilus*) dominated the biomass of our catches, comprising 32 and 28 percent of the total. Other taxa collected were bridgelip sucker (*Catostomus columbianus*), longnose dace (*Rhinichthys cataractae*), speckled dace (*Rhinichthys osculus*), white crappie (*Pomoxis nigromaculatus*), sculpins (*Cottus* sp.), chiselmouth (*Acrocheilus alutaceus*), mountain whitefish (*Prosopium williamsoni*), and bull trout.

Fish Catch per Unit Effort

Catch rates of fish in Beulah Reservoir varied greatly by season, year, and gear type. The overall CPUE of fyke nets for all species combined was highest during spring 2007 and spring 2006 (6.0–6.5 fish/h or FPH), lowest in fall 2007 and spring 2008 (1.2–1.5 FPH), and intermediate during fall 2006 (5.0 FPH; table 4). When we used gillnets, overall CPUE was highest in fall 2006 (10.6 FPH), lowest during springs 2006 and 2008 (about 1.8 FPH), and intermediate during spring (4.7 FPH) and fall 2007 (4.5 FPH; table 4).

Catch rates of fyke nets for dace ranged from 0.25 ± 0.56 FPH (mean $\pm$ SD) during spring 2006 to 0.01 ± 0.02 FPH during fall 2007 (fig. 13). Catch rates of dace during spring 2006 were 5–48 times higher than other study periods and significantly higher than catch rates in fall 2006 ($P < 0.001$). Pairwise comparisons of CPUE for other sample periods were not significant. Dace ≤50 mm comprised 76–83 percent of our fyke net catch before and about one-half of our catch after the reservoir was dewatered (fig. 14). The proportion of dace 51–70 mm collected increased by about 81–200 percent after the reservoir was dewatered. Dace >70 mm were more common during spring 2008 (7 percent of catch) than during all other periods (≤4 percent of catch). Dace were not captured by gillnets.

Catch rates of fyke nets for northern pikeminnow ranged from 2.90 ± 6.73 FPH during fall 2006 to 0.20 ± 0.41 FPH during fall 2007 and did not differ between sample periods (fig. 15). Catch rates of small northern pikeminnow (<156 mm, the size that would be suitable prey for bull trout) ranged from 2.89 ± 6.72 FPH during fall 2006 to 0.19 ± 0.39 FPH during fall 2007 and again did not differ between samples. The CPUE of these fish were 4–15 times higher before the reservoir was dewatered than after the reservoir was dewatered. Northern pikeminnow ≤100 mm represented most of catches (87–95 percent) for all sample periods (fig. 16). During spring 2006, the modal length of small pikeminnow (range = 61–65 mm) was greater than modal length from other years (range = 36–50 mm). Northern pikeminnow 101–200 mm comprised only 4–9 percent of the catches with fyke nets. The percentage of northern pikeminnow >200 mm in the catches was highest (about 9 percent of annual catch) immediately following dewatering (that is, fall 2007). When the reservoir refilled in spring 2008, large fish comprised less than 1 percent of the total catch. The catch rates of gillnets for all sizes of northern pikeminnow ranged from 6.09 ± 9.20 FPH during fall 2006 to 0.07 ± 0.36 FPH during fall 2007 (fig. 15). The catch rates of gillnets after reservoir dewatering (in summer 2007) were 63–99 percent lower than catch rates before dewatering. Total catch rates significantly increased from spring to fall 2006 ($P<0.001$) and decreased significantly from spring to fall 2007 ($P<0.001$). The CPUE of gillnets for smaller northern pikeminnow were highest during fall 2006 (2.65 ± 4.39 FPH) and nil after the reservoir was dewatered. The CPUE of gillnets for small northern pikeminnow significantly increased from spring to fall 2006 ($P <0.001$) and significantly decreased from fall 2006 to spring 2007 and from spring to fall 2007 ($P <0.01$; fig. 15). Prior to reservoir dewatering, fish from 101 to 200 mm comprised 70–93 percent of the catch by gillnet and they were not collected after the reservoir was dewatered (fig. 16). Northern pikeminnow >200 mm comprised from 7 percent (fall 2006) to 100 percent (fall 2007) of the catch by gillnet. Northern pikeminnow ≤100 mm were not collected by gillnets.

The CPUE of fyke nets for redside shiners ranged from 4.40 ± 9.81 FPH during spring 2007 to 0.74 ± 1.71 FPH during spring 2008 (fig. 17). Catch rates of redside shiners were 80–83 percent lower after the reservoir was dewatered when compared to rates before dewatering. Mean CPUE of redside shiners significantly decreased from spring to fall 2007 ($P<0.01$); all other pairwise comparisons did not differ. The modal lengths of redside shiners collected by fyke nets were higher for spring 2007 (56–60 mm) than modal lengths for other study periods (31–50 mm; fig. 18. Redside shiners ≤50 mm comprised from 28 percent (springs 2007 and 2008) to 88 percent (fall 2006) of the catch by fyke net. Redside shiners 51–70 mm were more common during spring 2007 (57 percent of total catch) than for other years (7–26 percent). Prior to dewatering of the reservoir, fish >70 mm comprised only 4–16 percent of the catch. After the reservoir was dewatered, fish >70 mm comprised 30–46 percent of the catch. When we used gillnets, mean CPUE of redside shiners ranged from 0.33 ± 1.17 FPH during spring 2007 to 0.02 ± 0.21 during spring 2008. Although CPUE decreased from 55 to 62 percent after the reservoir was dewatered (that is, from spring to fall 2007), no seasonal comparisons significantly differed. The sizes of redside shiners also were similar between sample periods (fig. 18).

Mean CPUE of fyke nets for suckers of all sizes ranged from 0.53 ± 1.22 FPH during spring 2007 to 0.06 ± 0.12 FPH during spring 2008 (fig. 19). Catch rates were 76–88 percent lower after the reservoir was dewatered when compared to rates before dewatering. Mean CPUE of all suckers significantly decreased from spring to fall 2007 ($P<0.001$). The catch rates of fyke nets for smaller suckers (<156 mm) ranged from 0.36 ± 1.19 FPH during spring 2007 to 0.02 ± 0.06 FPH during fall 2007. Mean CPUE for these smaller suckers significantly decreased from spring to fall 2006 ($P<0.05$; a 58-percent decrease) and from spring to fall 2007 ($P<0.001$; a 95- percent decrease). Immediately after the reservoir was dewatered, suckers ≤100 mm collected by fyke nets comprised only 14 percent of the catch compared to 47–67 percent of the catch during other periods (fig. 20). Suckers from 101 to 200 mm comprised 9 and 14 percent of the catch for fall 2006 and spring 2007, and 21–29 percent of the catch for other sample periods. The percentages of suckers >200 mm in the catches were highest immediately following dewatering (65 percent), lowest for spring 2006 (4 percent), and intermediate for other sample periods (24–36 percent). The CPUE of gillnets for all suckers ranged from 2.85 ± 3.41 FPH during fall 2007 to 0.20 ± 0.78 FPH during spring 2006 (fig. 19). Mean CPUE of gillnets for all suckers significantly differed ($P<0.001$) for all seasonal comparisons. Mean CPUE of gillnets for small suckers were low (<0.05 FPH) and did not differ between sample periods (fig. 19). Suckers ≤100 mm were collected only during spring 2006 (8 percent of their catch; fig. 20). Suckers 101–200 mm comprised 12–27 percent of the catch by gillnet before the reservoir was dewatered and only 0–3 percent of the catch after reservoir dewatering. Suckers >200 mm comprised most of the catch (73–100 percent) by gillnet and suckers were somewhat more common after the reservoir was dewatered (97–100 percent) compared to before reservoir dewatering (73–88 percent).

Mean CPUE of fyke nets for white crappie were highest during fall 2006 (0.14 ± 0.23 FPH) and spring 2007 (0.12 ± 0.24 FPH) and white crappie were not collected after the reservoir was dewatered (fig. 21). Mean CPUE of fyke nets for white crappie significantly increased from spring to fall 2006 ($P<0.001$) and significantly decreased from spring to fall 2007 ($P<0.001$). Prior to dewatering, white crappies 50–150 mm comprised 75–100 percent of the catch (fig. 22). Crappies 151–250 mm comprised 4 and 25 percent of the catch for spring 2007 and fall 2006, and they were not collected during spring 2006. Fish >250 mm were collected by fyke nets only during fall 2006 (1 percent of the catch). When we used gillnets, mean CPUE of white crappie was highest during fall 2006 (1.49 ± 3.39 FPH), nil during fall 2007 and spring 2008, and intermediate during spring 2007 (fig. 21). Mean CPUE of gillnets for white crappie significantly increased from spring to fall 2006 ($P<0.001$) and significantly decreased from fall 2006 to spring 2007 ($P<0.001$) and from spring to fall 2007 ($P<0.01$). White crappies from 50 to 150 mm comprised 93–100 percent of the catch by gillnet (fig. 22). Crappies from 151 to 250 mm were collected by gillnets only during fall 2006 (7 percent of catch) and fish >250 mm were not collected by this gear.

Fish Population Estimates

We estimated population abundance of different size cohorts of redside shiners, northern pikeminnow, and RBT in Beulah Reservoir during springs and falls 2006 and 2007 and spring 2008. Redside shiners and northern pikeminnow were the most abundant fish during all sample periods and their population estimates varied considerably between sample periods. All fish showed a substantial decrease in abundance following the reservoir dewatering in 2007.

Population estimates for all sizes of redside shiners were highest during spring sample periods (except for 2008) and lowest during the fall (fig. 23). Abundance was highest in the spring 2007 (198,313 ± 48,100) and lowest in the fall of the same year (14,777 ± 3,172). After a moderate reservoir drawdown during summer 2006, the population estimate for all sizes of redside shiners decreased by 44 percent from spring to fall (fig. 23). The magnitude of decrease was similar for juvenile (<68 mm; 43 percent) and adult fish (51 percent). After the reservoir was dewatered in summer 2007, the abundance of redside shiners in the fall was 93 percent lower than the abundance in the spring. Again, the magnitude of the decrease was similar for juvenile and adult fish. The population estimate for redside shiners of all sizes was 70 percent higher in spring 2008 (about 6 months after the reservoir was dewatered) than in fall 2007 (immediately after dewatering). Abundances of juvenile redside shiners were similar between fall 2007 and spring 2008 whereas the abundance of adult fish increased fourfold. Adult redside shiners represented about one-half of the total population during spring 2008, which was considerably higher than other periods where adults comprised 6–24 percent of the total.

Population estimates of northern pikeminnow that would be suitable prey for bull trout (that is, fish <156 mm) were highest during spring 2006 (80,881 ± 32,884) and lowest during fall 2007 (3,940 ± 2,497; fig. 23). Population sizes of all fish in spring 2006 were 2 to 20 times higher than other sample periods. After the moderate drawdown of Beulah Reservoir in summer 2006, the abundance of prey-sized northern pikeminnow in fall 2006 was 52 percent lower than the abundance from the previous spring and was about 15 percent lower in spring 2007 than fall 2006 (fig. 23). The population estimate for all sizes of northern pikeminnow after the reservoir was dewatered (fall 2007) was 88 percent lower than the estimate from spring 2007 (fig. 23). In spring 2008, the abundance of all sizes of northern pikeminnow was 66 percent higher than the abundance from fall 2007.

Population estimates for smaller RBT that would be suitable prey for bull trout were less precise because of low sample sizes and recapture rates (no estimate was derived for spring 2006). Estimates ranged from 6,321 ± 6,272 fish in spring 2008 to 1,920 ± 1,435 fish in spring 2007 (fig. 23). The estimate from fall 2006 was twice that from spring 2007, but the 95-percent CI almost entirely overlapped. The population size of RBT more than doubled after the reservoir was dewatered and increased by 53 percent from fall 2007 to spring 2008 (fig. 23).

Catch of Bull Trout

We did not catch any bull trout in 2006, but caught 5 fish during spring 2007, 3 in fall 2007, and 14 in spring 2008. In spring 2007, we caught 3 bull trout in the northwest and 2 in the southern region of the reservoir, soon after the start of irrigation withdrawal. Of the 3 fish we captured in fall 2007, 2 were recaptured once during our sampling and the third fish was originally tagged in spring 2007. Of the 14 bull trout we captured during spring 2008, we recaptured 3 of these fish once. All bull trout in 2008 were captured in the northern half of the reservoir. Bull trout collected during spring 2007 were <300 mm, whereas bull trout collected from fall 2007 were >300 mm (fig. 24). Bull trout collected during spring 2008 ranged in length from 261 to 476 mm. Mean (± SD) condition factors for bull trout were highest in fall 2007 (1.13 ± 0.08), lowest in spring 2008 (1.00 ± 0.09), and intermediate in spring 2007 (1.08 ± 0.10; fig. 25). All bull trout in 2007 had values of K greater than 1.00, but only 35 percent of fish collected in 2008 had K values exceeding 1. All bull trout that were recaptured in 2007 showed an increase in mass between captures (range 0.4–0.8 g/day), whereas fish that were recaptured during spring 2008 lost mass (range 1.2–2.0 g/day). Bull trout fed on invertebrates and fish during springs 2007 and 2008, and fed only on fish during fall 2007. Bull trout captured during 2007 (10 percent) and 2008 (70 percent) had less than 1 g of food in their stomachs.

Bioenergetics Modeling

Our simulations indicated that the per capita consumption of fish and invertebrates by bull trout was highest in spring, lowest in winter, and correlated with reservoir temperature (fig. 26). The growth rates used in our simulations had obvious effects on the total consumption by populations of 188 and 1,000 bull trout (table 5). For example, the predatory impact of a population of 188 bull trout with a diet comprised of only fish and a high growth rate (2.3 g/day) was over twice that of fish with a medium growth rate (0.64 g/day) and over five times greater than fish with a low growth rate (0.01 g/day; table 5).

The total consumption by a hypothetical population of 188 bull trout during our simulation period exceeded the available prey biomass in the fall 2006 (which we estimated was about 266 kg) when they consumed only fish and grew at a high rate (fig. 27). When their diet was comprised of fish and invertebrates, bull trout consumed from 19 to 96 percent of the available prey fish and from 14 to 120 percent of the prey fish when their diet was comprised of fish only. When we conducted simulations using a population of 1,000 bull trout, total consumption exceeded the available prey fish, depending on growth rate and regardless of diet composition (fig. 27). A population of 1,000 bull trout with a medium growth rate (0.64 g/day) eliminated their prey fish base on days 145–180 and those with a high growth rate (2.3 g/day) exhausted their prey on days 70–81. In contrast, bull trout with a low growth rate (0.01 g/day) exhausted their forage base when their diet was comprised of only fish (day 192).

In fall 2007, we estimated the biomass of available prey fish in Beulah Reservoir to be just 76 kg, or less than one-quarter of the value in 2006. The estimated total consumption by a population of 188 bull trout exceeded the available forage, depending on diet composition and growth rate (fig. 28). For a population of 188 bull trout, only those with a low growth rate (0.01 g/day) did not exhaust their prey fish base regardless of their diet composition. The number of days for a population of 188 bull trout to eliminate their prey for other diet and growth scenarios ranged from 113 to 181 days. When we conducted simulations using a population of 1,000 bull trout, total consumption exceeded the available prey fish base in every scenario we modeled (fig. 28). The number of days it required for 1,000 bull trout to eliminate their prey fish base ranged from 17 to 86 days, depending on diet composition and daily growth rate.

Discussion

The purpose of our research at Beulah Reservoir was twofold. First, we wanted to determine whether typical water-level management of Beulah Reservoir adversely affected the prey base (fish and invertebrates) for bull trout. Second, we wanted to determine whether changes to prey populations could adversely affect consumption and production by overwintering bull trout within the reservoir. Our results indicate that the effects of a summer drawdown on the aquatic community within Beulah Reservoir depended on the magnitude of the event. In 2006, where the drawdown was relatively mild compared to other years, we detected few changes in the fish community when comparing metrics from fish caught in the spring to fish caught in the fall. However, we did note that the densities of benthic insects in areas that were frequently dewatered were lower than those in areas that remain inundated, which could have implications for bull trout foraging. In 2007, Beulah Reservoir was drawn down to run-of-river levels and the amount of habitat available for fish and invertebrates after dewatering was <1 percent of habitat available at full pool and all deep-water habitat was eliminated. As such, the densities of pelagic and benthic invertebrates decreased, the abundance of some fish species decreased, the sizes of fish in the catches changed, and we estimated the biomass of prey fish in Beulah Reservoir in fall 2007 to be just 76 kg, or less than one-quarter of the value in 2006. Our bioenergetics modeling exercises suggested that the moderate drawdown of 2006 left enough prey fish in the fall to provide even a large (≤1,000) population of bull trout with, at the least, a maintenance ration of forage for overwintering. In contrast, the extreme drawdown of 2007 severely reduced the prey fish biomass available in the fall and our simulations indicated that consumption by even a modest population of bull trout could exceed the available forage. Collectively, our results indicate that current water-level management of Beulah Reservoir does affect the aquatic community and may affect the health and well-being of overwintering bull trout. As we mentioned earlier, the severity of effects would be dependent on the extent of drawdown, population size of bull trout, their diet composition, and perhaps other unknown factors. Because we only evaluated the effects of two levels of drawdown—one moderate and one extreme—we can not predict the effects of drawdowns that occur between the levels we studied. At the least, our results provide information that could help establish minimum pool levels in Beulah Reservoir for the maintenance of forage fish and bull trout.

Water-level management in Beulah Reservoir is similar to other reservoirs in the Western United States in that a summer drawdown typically begins in April and May and continues into September and early October. However, water-level fluctuations in Beulah Reservoir seem to be more severe than most other reservoirs (see www.usbr.gov/pn/hydromet, accessed February 27, 2009). Although this management strategy may facilitate providing irrigation water, it contrasts with a water management strategy for the benefit of fish, in which reservoirs would be full during spring and summer for growth and spawning of fish and reduced during winter (Hulsey, 1957). The wet winter of 2005–06 allowed Beulah Reservoir to fill earlier and stay full longer when compared to other years. This resulted in an early start to withdrawal (March) and water releases over the spillway, which may increase entrainment of fish through Agency Valley Dam (Schwabe and Tiley, 1999). The drier winter and spring 2007 led to a reduced reservoir volume and drafting that caused the reservoir to reach run-of-river levels on August 30. During this extreme drawdown, mortalities of fish upstream of the dam were not common (except for several suckers) but downstream of the dam, a large fish kill occurred. Because of the large number of fish involved in the die-off, we surmise that most of these fish were entrained and that some of the changes we saw in our fish population metrics after drawdown were due to entrainment. Capturing and moving some of these fish back to the reservoir, or installing a fish barrier at Agency Valley Dam, may offset some of these losses.

Water-quality variables differed between the spring and fall. The magnitude of drawdown in Beulah Reservoir had minor effects on water quality when comparing metrics in the spring to those in the fall. As such, changes in water quality after drawdown probably had little effect on fish health or well being. For example, we rarely recorded temperatures >15°C or DO concentrations <6.5 mg/L, which are threshold values considered suitable for bull trout (Rieman and McIntyre, 1993; Bureau of Reclamation, 2002). Most of the time, water temperatures in the reservoir and in the NFMR were less than the tolerance limits of other species, except on occasion for mountain whitefish and perhaps sculpin (Black, 1953; Scott and Crossman, 1973; Symons and others, 1976; Kaya, 1978; Castleberry and Cech, 1986; Eaton and others, 1995; Hillman and others, 1999; Selong and others, 2001). Despite the high productivity of Beulah Reservoir (Bureau of Reclamation, 2002), anaerobic conditions were not evident in the hypolimnion.

We observed considerable changes in water clarity between seasons and years at Beulah Reservoir. The decreases in mean Secchi depths from spring to fall were likely related to increases in primary production (Bureau of Reclamation, 2002) and to low reservoir volumes mixing with incoming and re-suspended sediments (Fox and others, 1977; Popp and Hoagland, 1995). The relatively low water clarity during spring 2006 may have resulted from increased sediment inputs from tributary streams (Popp and Hoagland, 1995) and from water being released over the spillway, which facilitates nutrient exchange from deeper, nutrient-rich waters and increases primary production (Murphy, 1962). The effects of changes in water turbidity on the behavior and foraging success of bull trout are unknown.

The drawdowns we studied in Beulah Reservoir resulted in lower densities of pelagic invertebrates, lower densities of chironomids in sediments that were frequently dewatered, and a smaller size of individuals in areas of frequent dewatering. All these changes could affect bull trout in the reservoir because invertebrates can be an important forage item for these fish at certain times of the year. For example, Wilhelm and others (1999) noted that the diet of bull trout (>250 mm) in high alpine lakes of the Canadian Rocky Mountains (where other fishes were not present) contained more than 90 percent chironomids following ice out. Beauchamp and Van Tassel (2001) reported that 69–88 percent of the diet of bull trout (200–400 mm) consisted of invertebrates from January to May in Lake Billy Chinook, Oregon. Our results showed that bull trout could consume substantial quantities of invertebrates, indicating that more detailed study of the effects of reservoir management on invertebrate populations is warranted. A detailed description of the aquatic invertebrates in Beulah Reservoir and the effects of drawdown on them were beyond the scope of our work.

Although the most common pelagic invertebrates we captured were Hydracarina and chironomids, our highest mean catch during any sample period was only 1.5 Hydracarina per m^3. We only caught relatively high numbers of Hydracarina in spring 2007—at all other times our catch was essentially nil. Our catches were on the low side of the range reported by other studies, which spanned from an "occasional event" to more than 100 individuals per m^3 (Gliwicz and Biesiadka, 1975; Riessen, 1982; Cassano and others, 2002). Because water mites are considered unpalatable for fish (Kerfoot, 1982), we do not know the influence that changes in their populations would have on overwintering bull trout in Beulah Reservoir. Our results, however, suggest that Hydracarina densities were severely reduced after the complete dewatering of 2007. For pelagic chironomids, we only captured them in relatively high numbers in springs 2006 and 2007—catches were essentially nil during other periods. Even so, our highest mean catch was only 0.5 individuals per m^3 and our catch rates decreased gradually from 2006 to 2007, suggesting that summer water-level manipulations, and perhaps other factors, were affecting chironomid populations. Our results also indicate that chironomid densities were severely reduced after the complete dewatering of 2007. In the fall, chironomids may have been subjected to increased predation due to high densities of predators and altered swimming behavior of the insects (Yamagishi and Fukuhara, 1971; Mousavi and others, 2002; Takagi and others, 2005).

We observed fewer and smaller chironomids in sediments of the reservoir that were frequently dewatered compared to areas that typically were inundated, which is similar to the results of Furey and others (2006). This may be because only some taxa of chironomids can tolerate short-term drying of the substrate (Fillion, 1967; Pinder, 1986). Because of the limited scope of our invertebrate sampling, we did not attempt to quantify annual losses of chironomids due to reservoir drawdown. Benson and Hudson (1975) found that reducing fall drawdown by 4–5 m yielded a three-fold increase in benthic macroinvertebrate production during May. For newly impounded reservoirs, colonization of the benthos by chironomids begins the summer following impoundment when their growth, reproduction, and dispersal are highest (Paterson and Fernando, 1969; Voshell and Simmons, 1984). Similarly, our results suggest that recolonization of the benthos by chironomids occurs the summer after Beulah Reservoir is dewatered and that the amount of biomass available for bull trout is low during late fall and winter following a dewatering event. More study is needed to understand the relation between chironomid density in the benthos, their densities in open water, and the influence of summer drawdowns.

Despite the reduction of nearshore habitat available for fish in the fall, our catches of fish in fyke nets were similar between spring and fall 2006, indicating that fish densities did not change appreciably during a year of moderate drawdown. In 2007, however, which included a complete dewatering of the reservoir, catch rates of most species significantly decreased from spring to fall. Our results suggest that moderate reductions in water volume (1) do not elicit widespread emigration of fish from the reservoir, (2) concentrates fish in offshore areas, and (3) leads to stable or even increased catch rates of many species of fish. For example, the catch rates by gillnet of northern pikeminnow, suckers, and white crappie all increased in fall 2006. In contrast, complete dewatering events may lead to large-scale emigrations of fish upstream and downstream. Although we did not sample the river upstream of the reservoir, the fish kill that occurred downstream of Agency Valley Dam late in summer 2007 indicates that many fish left the reservoir. Although sampling was more difficult in the run-of-river conditions left after dewatering, the low densities of fish probably were real and not an artifact of sampling because poor catch rates persisted into spring 2008. This indicates that fish density remained low and that limited recovery of the fish community occurred over the winter. Because we only evaluated two levels of drawdown in Beulah Reservoir and the response of different species to these manipulations varies, it is difficult to ascribe clear cause-effect relations between drawdown, water volume, and fish abundance. Our results indicate that higher reservoir levels and increased shoreline cover from spring through fall improves the overwinter survival of many fishes or that immigration of fish into the reservoir from tributaries increases when river flows were higher. Miranda and others (1984) and Willis (1986) suggested that higher reservoir levels and increased shoreline cover improve survival for subyearling largemouth bass (*Micropterus salmoides*).

Besides affecting the overall catch rates of some species, water-level management in Beulah Reservoir had obvious effects on the sizes of fish in the reservoir. Specifically, the dewatering event of 2007 severely reduced the numbers of all sizes of dace, northern pikeminnow <200 mm, redside shiners from 20 to 65 mm, and suckers of all sizes. The severe drawdown completely eliminated white crappie. Our results indicate that the effects of a single dewatering in Beulah Reservoir occur quickly and can be dramatic. The drastic changes in water levels probably lowered the reproductive success of fishes by dewatering eggs and larvae, reducing the amount of spawning substrate, and exposing juveniles to increased predation (Lantz and others, 1967; Heman and others, 1969; Estes, 1972; Willis, 1986). Some fish, however, seemed a bit more resilient to the dewatering event of 2007. For example, our catch rates of juvenile dace increased in spring 2008, indicating that these fish may have persisted in tributaries while the reservoir was dewatered and they moved into the reservoir after it started to refill. Indeed, Gonzalez and others (1998) documented downstream migrations of dace in the NFMR upstream of Beulah Reservoir during fall. The presence of larger-sized native fishes, like suckers, also suggests that these fish show some resilience to reservoir dewatering.

Although our results clearly indicate that a single dewatering event can negatively affect fish populations in Beulah Reservoir, some evidence suggests that the effects may be short lived. For example, our catch rates of fish in 2006 and spring 2007 and the sizes of fish represented in those catches were indicative of robust populations with diverse age structures. In particular, most individuals collected were smaller and consisted of a high proportion of subyearling fish. Our work in 2006 was conducted about 1.5–2.5 years after consecutive dewatering events in Beulah Reservoir from 2002 to 2004. Petersen and Kofoot (2002) and Petersen and others (2003) sampled Beulah Reservoir during summers 2001 and 2002—prior to the 3 consecutive years of dewatering—and also reported that diverse age structures of fish were present. Thus, if severe drawdown events were having lasting effects on prey fish populations in Beulah Reservoir, we would have expected some evidence of this when we started sampling in 2006. However, the reasons why our catches in 2006 were high and contained many small fish could be due to higher reproductive success from adults that persisted in the reservoir, increased recruitment in a relatively predator-free post-dewatering environment, and emigration of fishes from areas upstream of the reservoir. In 2006, there also was increased shoreline cover and spawning areas available for fish at the higher pool levels, which is important for fish production (Stroud, 1948; Johnson, 1963; Scott and Crossman, 1973; Nelson and Walburg, 1977; Martin and others, 1981). Paller (1997) documented similar increases in smaller individuals and decreases in larger individuals of various warm water species after a 4-year drawdown of Par Pond, South Carolina. In the end, documenting the long-term effects of a single drawdown or multiple, consecutive drawdowns on fish populations was beyond the scope of our study. We found that about 8 months after a complete dewatering event, many aspects of the fish populations in Beulah Reservoir change substantially, including relative abundance, absolute abundance, and size structure. We also noted that high catch rates of fish with diverse size structures are possible in Beulah Reservoir about 1.5 years after three consecutive dewatering events. However, we have little context to interpret this information. Based on a review of gillnet catch data from 1955 to 1970, Petersen and others (2003) also concluded that reservoir dewatering does not cause long-term changes to the fish community in Beulah Reservoir. Sampling of the fish populations in Beulah Reservoir in the absence of moderate or severe drawdowns would provide information on the natural seasonal variability of selected metrics and a baseline for understanding the effects of drawdown.

Our estimates of population size for most species were limited by our ability to recapture fish. Therefore, we only estimated abundance for the species that were most common and consistently recaptured, including redside shiners, northern pikeminnow, and RBT. The moderate drawdown of 2006 may have affected populations of redside shiners and northern pikeminnow, both of which had higher abundance in the spring than in the fall. However, there are many possible explanations for this change in population size, including an influx of subyearling fishes from tributaries during late fall and early winter, changes in vulnerability of fish to the gear, losses due to predation, outmigration of larger fishes, and direct losses due to the drawdown. Although abundance estimates were lower during the fall, fish biomass may continue to increase from the fall through spring if over-winter growth occurs. In contrast, the dewatering of the reservoir in 2007 reduced the populations of northern pikeminnow and redside shiners by more than 90 percent. Population estimates for RBT, however, were higher after dewatering than before dewatering. Gonzalez and others (1998) documented downstream migrations of wild RBT in the NFMR during fall through spring and perhaps some RBT migrated into Beulah Reservoir during fall, avoided entrainment, and dealt with the stressful conditions associated with the dewatering. As such, the effects of dewatering on RBT populations may not be evident until several years later, when reductions in adult population size may result in limited recruitment. The situation with RBT in Beulah Reservoir is even more confusing considering the planting of hatchery fish that occurs most springs (table 6). Because RBT could potentially compete with bull trout for resources in Beulah Reservoir, the ecology and biology of RBT warrant further study.

The dewatering of Beulah Reservoir and the resultant changes in prey populations may have had some effects on bull trout. Of all the bull trout we captured in Beulah Reservoir, only fish from spring 2008 had condition factors lower than 1.0. The mean condition factor of bull trout in Beulah Reservoir during spring 2008 also was 17 percent lower than that of similar sized fish from Lake Billy Chinook, Oregon (Beauchamp and Van Tassell, 2001). Given the decreases in abundance of fish following the dewatering event of 2007, it seems plausible that prey availability for bull trout in the winter 2007 and spring 2008 was sparse, perhaps resulting in lower fish conditions. Furthermore, the extent of reservoir drawdown is correlated with the estimated spawning population size of bull trout in the NFMR (fig. 29; Schwabe and others, 2006). However, sampling bull trout was not a focus of our study, sample sizes were low, and more information is needed to confirm any notions about prey availability, condition of bull trout, and the effects of water-level management on their health and well being.

Our bioenergetics modeling simulations suggested that current water-level management could limit bull trout production in Beulah Reservoir and the NFMR. Our analysis revealed that under a moderate drawdown, there probably would be enough prey fish in the fall to support a large population of bull trout under some growth and diet scenarios. After a complete dewatering of the reservoir, however, predation by even a modest population of bull trout could exceed or remove a high proportion of the prey biomass. The key variables determining the extent of predator impact in Beulah Reservoir were the biomass of prey available in the fall, the number of bull trout inhabiting the reservoir, diet composition of bull trout, and their growth rate. Of these, we had empirical data on prey biomass, and the diet and growth of bull trout to base our simulations on. We did not know how many bull trout actually used the reservoir for overwintering and modeled two hypothetical populations based on recovery criteria. Obviously, this was a key variable in our bioenergetics analysis and is an area of study for future research. Because of the possibility that bull trout can deplete their forage base, dewatering of Beulah Reservoir may adversely affect the health and well-being of bull trout.

There are several ways to improve our bioenergetics analysis. First, as we just alluded to, more information is needed on the number and percentage of bull trout of all sizes in the NFMR that actually use Beulah Reservoir during certain times. This probably is the biggest gap in our knowledge of the potential predatory impact of bull trout in Beulah Reservoir and is fundamental for evaluating the adequacy of the forage base. Such information also would help define the life history of bull trout in the NFMR and could be useful for establishing recovery criteria. For example, if substantial numbers of resident bull trout exist in the NFMR, then a recovery criterion based on adult population size (for example, 1,000–1,500 fish; U.S. Fish and Wildlife Service, 2002) could be distributed amongst interconnected populations. We also need more information on the activity, diet, feeding rates, and growth of bull trout from fall through spring to parameterize the model with relevant data from the field. For example, we used diet information and growth data from only a small number of individuals and were not able to partition diet data into size cohorts or describe temporal variation with much detail. Evaluating the predatory impact of other species, particularly northern pikeminnow and redband trout, would provide a more thorough understanding of predator-prey interactions in Beulah Reservoir and potential effects of reservoir management on bull trout. Clearly, bull trout predation does not occur in a vacuum and a more thorough, food-web based analysis would be more informative and useful. Finally, evaluating recruitment of prey fish during the simulation period would provide a better depiction of prey dynamics within the reservoir. Addressing these, and perhaps other, issues about bull trout and their prey in the NFMR basin would not only improve model results, but it also would allow for more informed decision making regarding reservoir operations and species recovery.

Summary

The overall goal of our research was to evaluate the effects of seasonal drawdowns on measures of insect and fish production in Beulah Reservoir. We wanted to use this information to determine a pool level, or volume, in Beulah Reservoir to maintain after drawdown to ensure adequate forage for bull trout that may overwinter in the reservoir. In 2 consecutive years, we evaluated the effects of a moderate (about a 68-percent decrease in pool volume) drawdown and a complete dewatering of Beulah Reservoir and concluded that adequate forage for bull trout would exist after the moderate but not the severe drawdown. The complete dewatering, and to a lesser extent the moderate drawdown, resulted in decreases in the abundance of pelagic and benthic invertebrates, the relative abundance and biomass of several species of fish, the absolute abundance of northern pikeminnow and redside shiners, and changes in the size and species composition of our catches. These changes were evident at least 8 months after the dewatering event and we do not know how long it will take fish and insect populations to recover. Based on bioenergetics modeling simulations, we hypothesize that the forage fish populations remaining after a moderate drawdown would be sufficient for a large population of bull trout under several growth and diet scenarios. After a complete dewatering, however, there would be inadequate time for forage fish populations to recover and the biomass of prey would be insufficient for even a modest overwintering population of bull trout.

Because we sampled Beulah Reservoir before and after only two drawdown events, we can not determine the minimum pool volume needed to sustain a suitable forage fish population for bull trout. Continued monitoring of fish populations in Beulah Reservoir over a wider range of drawdown scenarios, particularly moderate to high levels, would increase our understanding of the effects of reservoir operations and may allow for minimum pool recommendations. In addition, because of their importance to the diet of bull trout, more detailed information on the responses of aquatic insect populations to drawdown in Beulah Reservoir would be prudent. Finally, and perhaps most importantly, detailed study of the movements, distribution, habitat use, and general life history of bull trout in the NFMR and Beulah Reservoir are needed to develop recommendations for water management of the reservoir.

Acknowledgments

We thank Katy Hanna, Alexis Koenings, and Joseph Mullins for their invaluable assistance in the field and during data processing. Tim Walters and Ray Perkins from Oregon Department of Fish and Wildlife, and Lawrence Schwabe and Jason Fenton of the Department of Fish and Wildlife of the Burns Paiute Tribe, provided field gear and technical advice. This manuscript benefited from the careful peer review of Tim Walters, Sally Sauter, and biologists from the Bureau of Reclamation.

References Cited

Bayley, P.B., and Osborne, L.L., 1993, Natural rehabilitation of stream fish populations in an Illinois catchment: Freshwater Biology, v. 29, p. 295-300.

Beauchamp, D.A., LaRiviere, M.G., and Thomas, G.L., 1995, Evaluation of competition and predation as limits to juvenile kokanee and sockeye salmon production in Lake Washington: North American Journal of Fisheries Management, v. 15, p. 193-207.

Beauchamp, D.A., and Van Tassell, J.J., 2001, Modeling seasonal trophic interactions of adfluvial bull trout in Lake Billy Chinook, Oregon: Transactions of the American Fisheries Society, v. 130, p. 204-216.

Benson, N.G., and Hudson, P.L., 1975, Effects of a reduced fall drawdown on benthos abundance in Lake Francis Case: Transactions of the American Fisheries Society, v. 104, p. 526-528.

Black, E.C., 1953, Upper lethal temperatures of some British Columbia Fishes: Journal of the Fisheries Research Board of Canada, v. 10, p. 196-200.

Bureau of Reclamation, 2002, Beulah Reservoir water quality modeling study: Vale Irrigation Project, Oregon, Denver, Colorado.

Cassano, C.R., Castilho-Noll, M.S.M., and Arcifa, M.S., 2002, Water mite predation on zooplankton of a tropical lake: Brazilian Journal of Biology, v. 62, no. 4a, p. 565-571.

Castleberry, D.T., and Cech, J.J., 1986, Physiological-responses of a native and introduced desert fish to environmental stressors: Ecology, v. 67, p. 912-918.

Eaton, J.G., McCormick, J.H., Goodno, B.E., O'Brien, D.G., Stefan, H.G., Hondzo, M., and Scheller R.M., 1995, A field information-based system for estimating fish temperature tolerances: Fisheries, v. 20, no. 4, p. 10-18.

Estes, R.D., 1972, Ecological impact of fluctuating water levels in reservoirs, *in* Hoffman, D.A., ed., Ecological impact of water resource development: a technical session of the symposium, "Water, man, nature": Washington, D.C., Bureau of Reclamation.

Fillion, D.B., 1967, The abundance and distribution of benthic fauna of three mountain reservoirs on the Kananskis River in Alberta: Journal of Applied Ecology, v. 4, no. 1, p. 1-11.

Fox, J.L., Brezonick, P.L., and Kerin, M.A., 1977, Lake drawdown as a method of improving water quality: Washington D.C., U.S. Environmental Protection Agency, 93 p.

Fraley, J.J., and Shepard, B.B., 1989, Life history, ecology, and population status of migratory bull trout (*Salvelinus confluentus*) in the Flathead Lake and River System, Montana: Northwest Science, v. 63, p. 133-143.

Furey, P.C., Nordin, R.N., and Mazumberm, A., 2006, Littoral benthic macroinvertebrates under contrasting drawdown in a reservoir and a lake: Journal of the North American Benthological Society, v. 25, no. 1, p. 19-31.

Gaboury, M.N., and Patalas, J.W., 1984, Influence of water-level drawdown on the fish populations of Cross Lake, Manitoba: Canadian Journal of Fisheries and Aquatic Sciences, v. 41, p. 118-125.

Gliwicz, Z.M., and Biesiadka, E., 1975, Pelagic mites (Hydracarina) and their effect on the plankton community in a neo-tropical man-made lake: Arch. Hydrobiologia, v. 76, p. 65-88.

Gonzalez, D., 1998, Evaluate the life history of salmonids in the Malheur River Basin: Portland, Oregon, Annual Report to the Bonneville Power Administration.

Graham, P., Penkal, R., McMullin, S., Schladweiler, P., Mayes, H., Riggs, V., and Klaver, R.W., 1981, Montana: Recommendations for fish and wildlife program: Portland, Oregon, prepared for Pacific Northwest Electric Council.

Heman M.L., Cambell, R.S., and Redmond, L.C., 1969, Manipulation of fish populations through reservoir drawdown: Transaction of the American Fisheries Society, v. 2, p. 293–304.

Hillman, T.W., Miller, M.D., and Nishitani, B.A., 1999, Evaluation of seasonal-cold-water temperature criteria: Boise, Idaho, Idaho Division of Environmental Quality.

Howmiller, P.P., 1972, Effects of preservatives on weights of some common macrobenthic invertebrates: Transactions of the American Fisheries Society, v. 101, no. 4, p. 7433–7746.

Hulsey, A.H., 1957, Effects of a fall and winter drawdown on a flood control lake: Proceedings of the Annual Conference Southeastern Association of Game and Fish Commissioners, p. 285–289.

Johnson, R.P., 1963, Studies on the life history and ecology of the bigmouth buffalo, *Ictiobus cyprinellus* (*Valenciennes*): Journal of the Fisheries Research Board of Canada, v. 20, p. 1397–1429.

Kaya, C.M., 1978, Thermal resistance of rainbow trout from a permanently heated stream, and of two hatchery strains: The Progressive Fish-Culturist, v. 4, p. 138-142.

Kerfoot, W.C., 1982, A question of taste: crypsis and warning coloration in freshwater zooplankton communities: Ecology, v. 63, no. 2, p. 538–554.

Lagler, K.F., 1956, Freshwater Fishery Biology: Dubuque, Iowa, W.M.C. Brown.

Lantz, K.E., Davis, J.T., Hughes, J.S., and Schafer, H.E., Jr., 1967, Water level fluctuation—its effects on vegetation control and fish population management: Proceedings of the Annual Conference Southeastern Association of Game and Fish Commissioners, v. 18, p. 483–494.

Luecke, C., and Brandt, D., 1993, Estimating the energy density of daphnid prey for use with rainbow trout bioenergetics models: Transactions of the American Fisheries Society, v. 122, p. 386–389.

Malheur Watershed Council and Burns Piute Tribe, 2004, Malheur River Subbasin assessment and management plan for fish and wildlife mitigation, Appendix A, Part 2 Assessment Aquatic: Portland, Oregon, Northwest Power and Conservation Council.

Martin, D.B., Mengel, L.J., Novotny, J.F., and Walburg, C.H., 1981, Spring and summer water levels in a Missouri River Reservoir: Effects on age-0 fish and zooplankton: Transactions of the American Fisheries Society, v. 110, p. 370–381.

Matthews, W.J., 1986, Fish faunal structure in an Ozark stream: stability, persistence, and a catastrophic flood: Copeia, v. 1986, p. 388–397.

Mesa, M.G., Sauter, S.T., Phelps, J., and Petersen, J.H., 2007, Development of a bioenergetic model for bull trout: Longview, WA, report to U.S. Fish and Wildlife Service.

Miranda, L.E., Shelton, W.L., and Bryce, T.D., 1984, Effects of water level manipulation on abundance, mortality, and growth of young-of-year largemouth bass in West Point Reservoir, Alabama: North American Journal of Fisheries Management, v. 4, p. 314–320.

Mousavi, S.K., Sandring, S., and Amundsen, P., 2002, Diversity of chironomid assemblages in contrasting subarctic lakes–impact of fish predation and lake size: Archiv Fur Hydrobiologie, v. 154, p. 461–484.

Muhlfeld, C.C., Glutting, S., Hunt, R., Daniels, D., and Marotz, B., 2003, Winter diel habitat use and movement by subadult bull trout in the Upper Flathead River, Montana: North American Journal of Fisheries Management, v. 23, p. 163–171.

Murphy, G.I., 1962, Effect of mixing depth and turbidity on the productivity of fresh-water impounds: Transactions of the American Fisheries Society, v. 91, p. 69–76.

Nelson, W.R., and Walburg, C.H., 1977, Population dynamics of yellow perch (*Perca flavescens*), sauger (*Stizostedion canadense*), and walleye (*Stizostedion vitreum*) in four main stem Missouri River reservoirs: Journal of the Fisheries Research Board of Canada, v. 34, p. 1748–1763.

Nichols, S.A., 1975, The impact of over winter drawdown on the aquatic vegetation of the Chippewa Flowage, Wisconsin, USA: Transactions of the Wisconsin Academy of Sciences, Arts, and Letters, v. 63, p. 176–186.

Nielsen, L.A., and Johnson, D.L., 1983, Fisheries Techniques: Bethesda, MD, American Fisheries Society.

Paller, M.H., 1997, Recovery of a reservoir fish community from drawdown related impacts: North American Journal of Fisheries Management, v. 17, p. 726–733.

Paterson, C.G., and Fernando, C.H., 1969, The macroinvertebrate colonization of a small reservoir in Eastern Canada: Verb. Int. Ver. Limnology, v. 17, no. 126–136.

Pechen, G.A., 1965, Produktsiya vetvistousykh rakoobraznykh ozernogo zooplanktona, *in* Edmondson, W.T., and Winberg, G.G., eds., A manual on methods for the assessment of secondary productivity in fresh waters: London, England, International Biological Programme.

Petersen, J.H., and Kofoot, E.E., 2002, Conditions for growth and survival of bull trout in Beulah Reservoir, Oregon: Boise, Idaho, 2001 Annual Report to the Bureau of Reclamation, Pacific Northwest Region.

Petersen, J.H., Kofoot, E.E., and Rose, B., 2003, Conditions for growth and survival of bull trout in Beulah Reservoir, Oregon: Boise, Idaho, 2002 Annual Report to the Bureau of Reclamation, Pacific Northwest Region.

Pinder, L.C.V., 1986, Biology of freshwater Chironomidae: Annual Review of Entomology, v. 31, no. 1–23.

Popp, A., and Hoagland, K.D., 1995, Changes in benthic community composition in response to reservoir aging: Hydrobiologia, v. 306, p. 159-171.

Ratliff, D.E., and Howell, P.J., 1992, The status of bull trout populations in Oregon, *in* Howell, P.J., and Buchanan, D.V., eds., Proceedings of the Gearhart Mountain bull trout workshop: Oregon Chapter of the American Fisheries Society, p. 10-17.

Rieman, B.E., and McIntyre, J.D., 1993, Demographic and habitat requirements for conservation of bull trout: Ogden, Utah, U.S. Department of Agriculture, Forest Service, Intermountain Research.

Riessen, H.P., 1982, Pelagic water mites: their life history and seasonal distribution in the zooplankton community of a Canadian lake: Arch. Hydrobiologia Supp., v. 62, p. 410–439.

Rose, B.P., and Mesa, M.G., 2007, Bull trout forage investigations in Beulah Reservoir, Oregon. 2006 Annual Report: Boise, Idaho, Bureau of Reclamation.

Schneider, J.C., 1998, Lake fish population estimates by mark-and-recapture methods, chap. 8 *of* Schneider, J.C., ed., Manual of fisheries survey methods II: with periodic updates: Ann Arbor, Michigan, Michigan Department of Natural Resources, Fisheries Special Report 25.

Schwabe, L., Fenton, J., Perkins, R.R., DeHaan, P., Diggs, M., and Arden, W., 2006, Evaluation of the life history of native salmonids in the Malheur subbasin: Portland, Oregon, Annual Report to the Bonneville Power Administration Project 19701900.

Schwabe, L., and Tiley, M., 1999, Evaluation of the life history of native salmonids in the Malheur River basin: Portland, Oregon, Annual Report to the Bonneville Power Administration Project 9701900/9701901.

Scott, W.B., and Crossman, E.J., 1973, Freshwater fishes of Canada: Fisheries Research Board of Canada Bulletin 184.

Selong, J.H., McMahon, T.E., Zale, A.V., and Barrows, F.T., 2001, Effect of temperature on growth and survival of bull trout, with applications of an improved method for determining thermal tolerance in fishes: Transactions of the American Fisheries Society, v. 130, p. 1026–1037.

Sokal, R.R., and Rohlf, J.R., 2003, Biometry third edition: New York, W.H. Freeman and Company.

Stewart, D.J., Weininger, D., Rottiers, D.V., and Edsall, T.A., 1983, An energetic model for lake trout *Salvelinus namaycush*: application to the Lake Michigan population: Canadian Journal of Fisheries and Aquatic Sciences, v. 40, p. 681-698.

Stroud, R.H., 1948, Growth of the basses and black crappies in Norris Reservoir, Tennessee: Journal of Tennessee Academy of Science, v. 23, no. 1, p. 31–99.

Symons, P.E.K., Metcalfe, J.L., and Harding, G.D., 1976, Upper lethal and preferred temperatures of the slimy sculpin, *Cottus cognatus*: The Journal of the Fisheries Research Board of Canada, v. 33, no. 180–183.

Takagi, S., Kikuchi, E., Doi, H., and Shikano, S., 2005, Swimming behavior of *Chironomus acerbiphilus* larvae in Lake Katanuma: Hydrobiologia, v. 548, p. 153–165.

U.S. Fish and Wildlife Service, 2002, Malheur Recovery Unit, Oregon, chap. 14 *of* U.S. Fish and Wildlife Service: Portland, Oregon, Bull Trout (*Salvelinus confluentus*) Draft Recovery Plan, 71 p.

Voshell, J.R., and Simmons, G.M., Jr., 1984, Colonization and succession of macroinvertebrates in a new reservoir: Hydrobiologia, v. 112, p. 27-39.

Wilhelm, F.M., Parker, B.R., Schindlerm, D.W., and Donald, D.B., 1999, Seasonal food habits of bull trout from a small alpine lake in Canadian Rocky Mountains: Transactions of the American Fisheries Society, v. 128, p. 1176-1192.

Willis, D.W., 1986, Review of water level management of Kansas reservoirs, *in* Hall, G.E., and Van Den Avyle, M.J., eds., Reservoir fisheries management: strategies for the 80s: Bethesda, Maryland, American Fisheries Society, Southern Division, Reservoir Committee, p. 110-114.

Woods, P.F., and Falter, C.M., 1982, Limnological investigations: Lake Koocanusa, Montana. Part 4: Factors controlling primary productivity. Special report 82–15: Seattle District, Seattle, U.S. Army Corps of Engineers.

Yamagishi, H., and Fukuhara, H., 1971, Note on the swimming behavior of *Chironomus plumosus* larvae in Lake Suwa: Japanese Journal of Ecology, v. 20, p. 256-257.

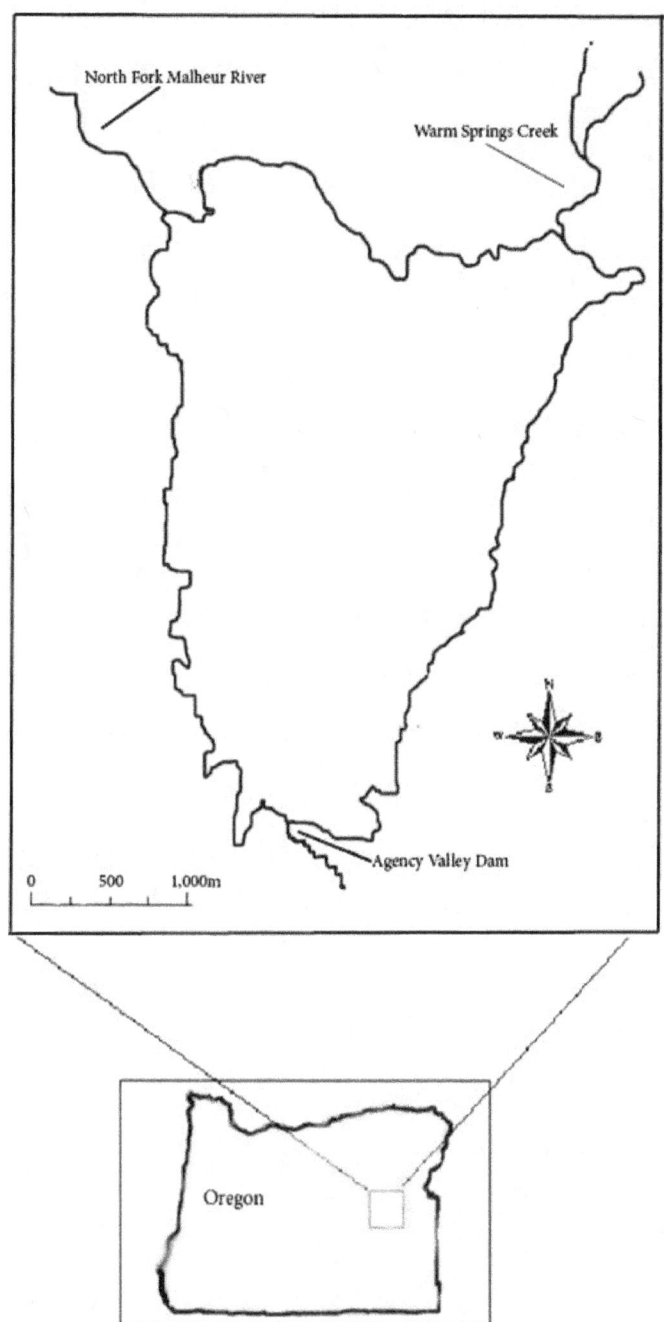

Figure 1. Map showing general location and tributaries of Beulah Reservoir, Oregon.

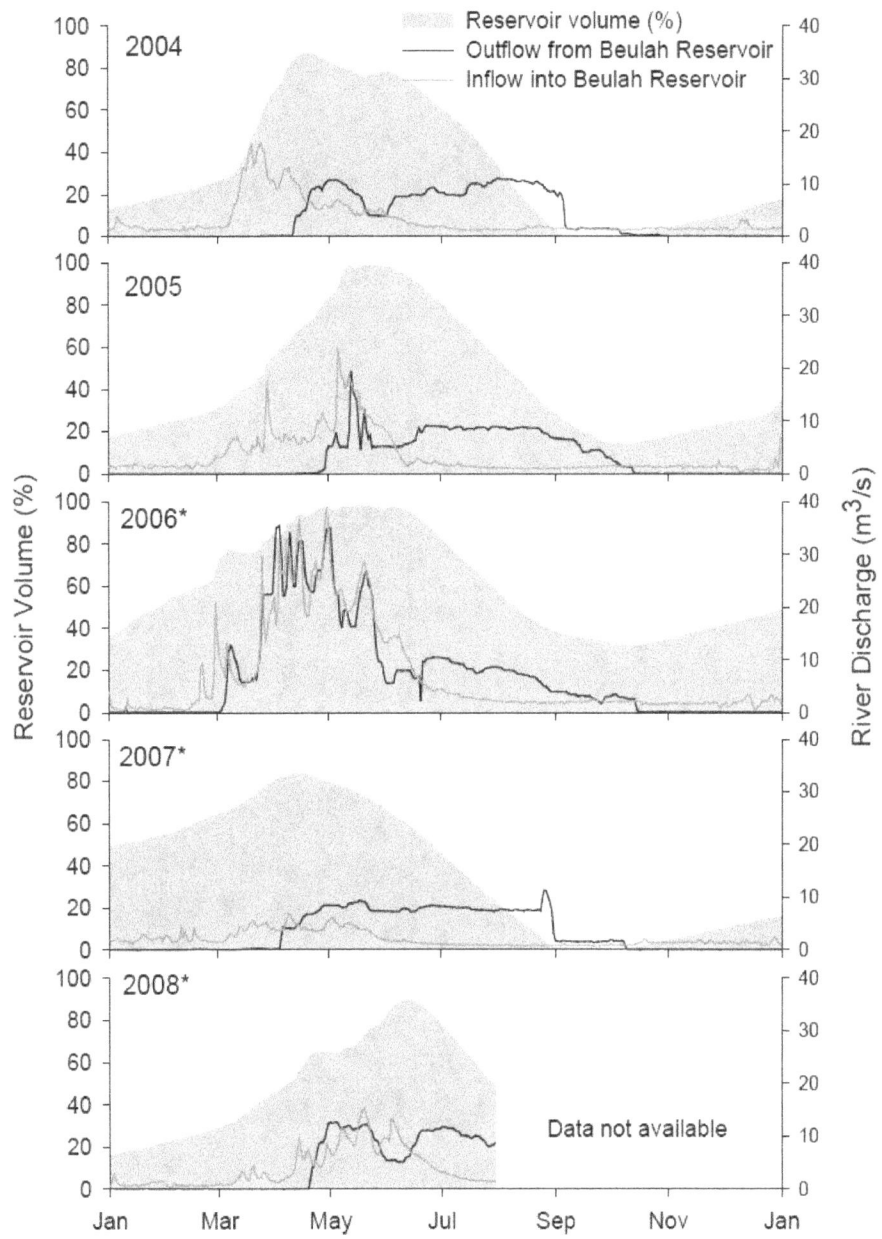

Figure 2. Discharge of water entering and exiting Beulah Reservoir and reservoir volume, 2004–08. Our study occurred during years marked with an asterisk.

Figure 3. Photographs of a fish kill that occurred downstream of Agency Valley Dam on the North Fork of the Malheur River during the fall of 2007 after the end of irrigation season and the release of water. By November, the fish kill extended about 500 m downstream Photograph taken by Brien P Rose, USGS, November 2007).

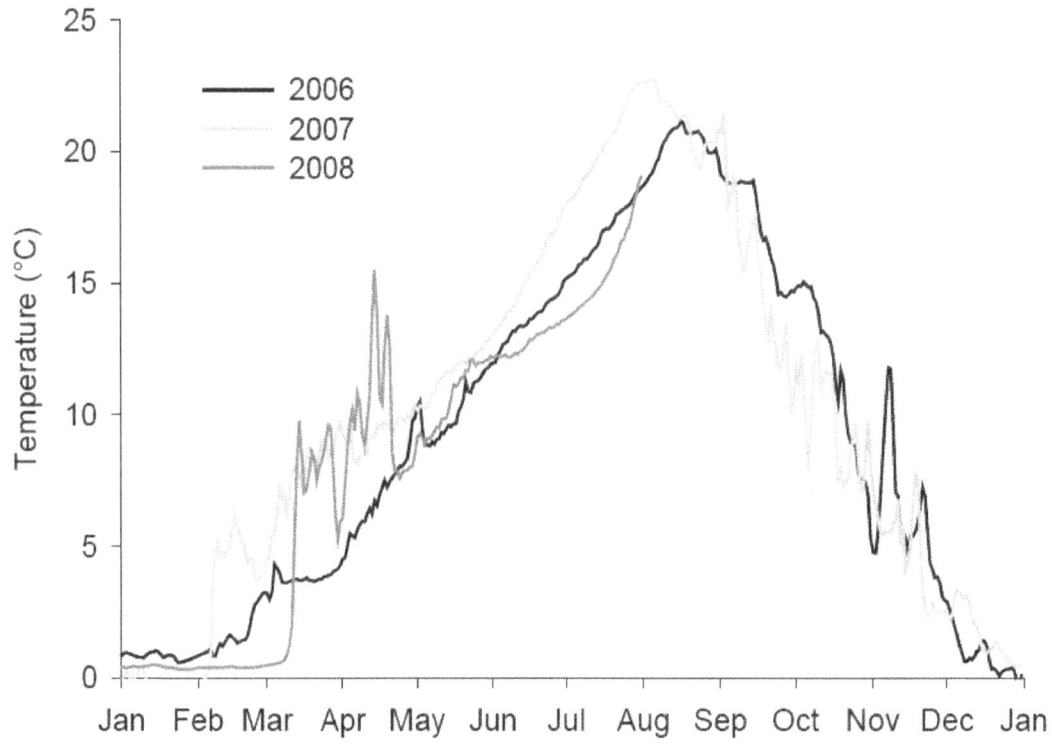

Figure 4. Mean daily temperatures at the outflow of Beulah Reservoir, 2006–08.

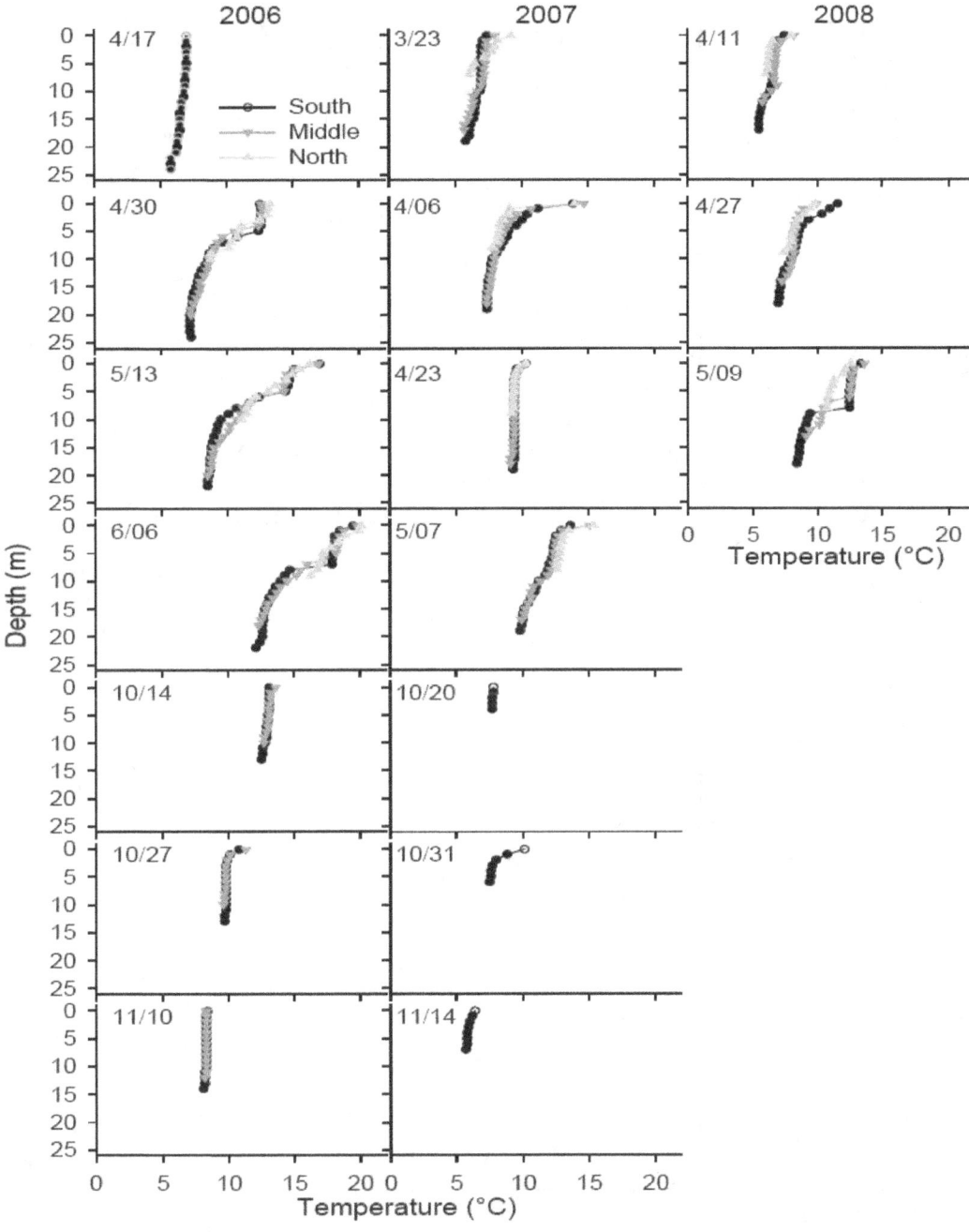

Figure 5. Water-temperature profiles in three regions of Beulah Reservoir, 2006–08. The length of each profile corresponds to depths of the reservoir for each period. The middle and north sites were not sampled on April 17, 2006, and data were not collected at some sites due to insufficient water depths or because the sites were dry.

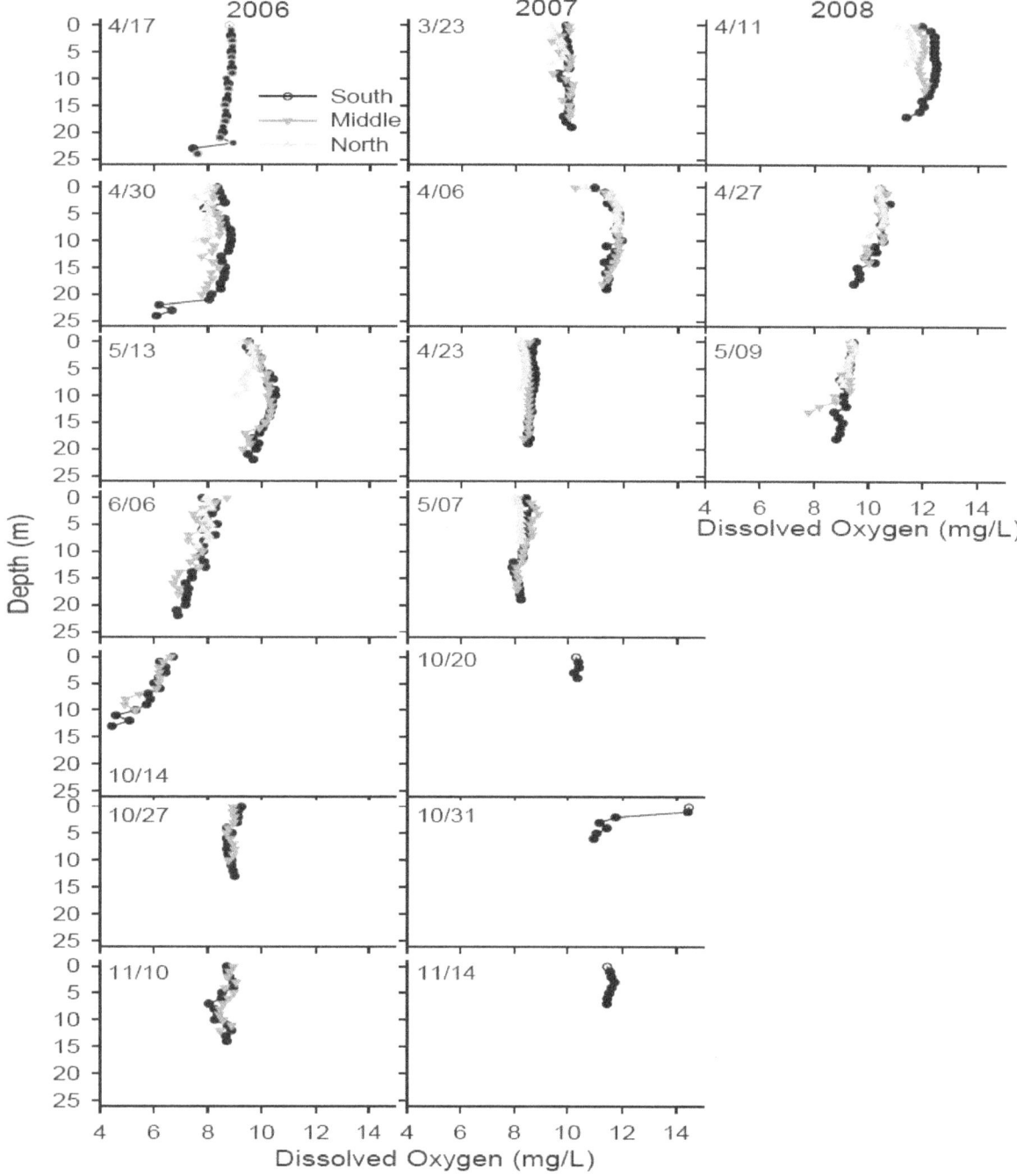

Figure 6. Dissolved-oxygen profiles in three regions of Beulah Reservoir, 2006–08. The length of each profile corresponds to depths of the reservoir for each period. The middle and north sites were not sampled on April 17, 2006, and data were not collected at some sites due to insufficient water depths or because the sites were dry.

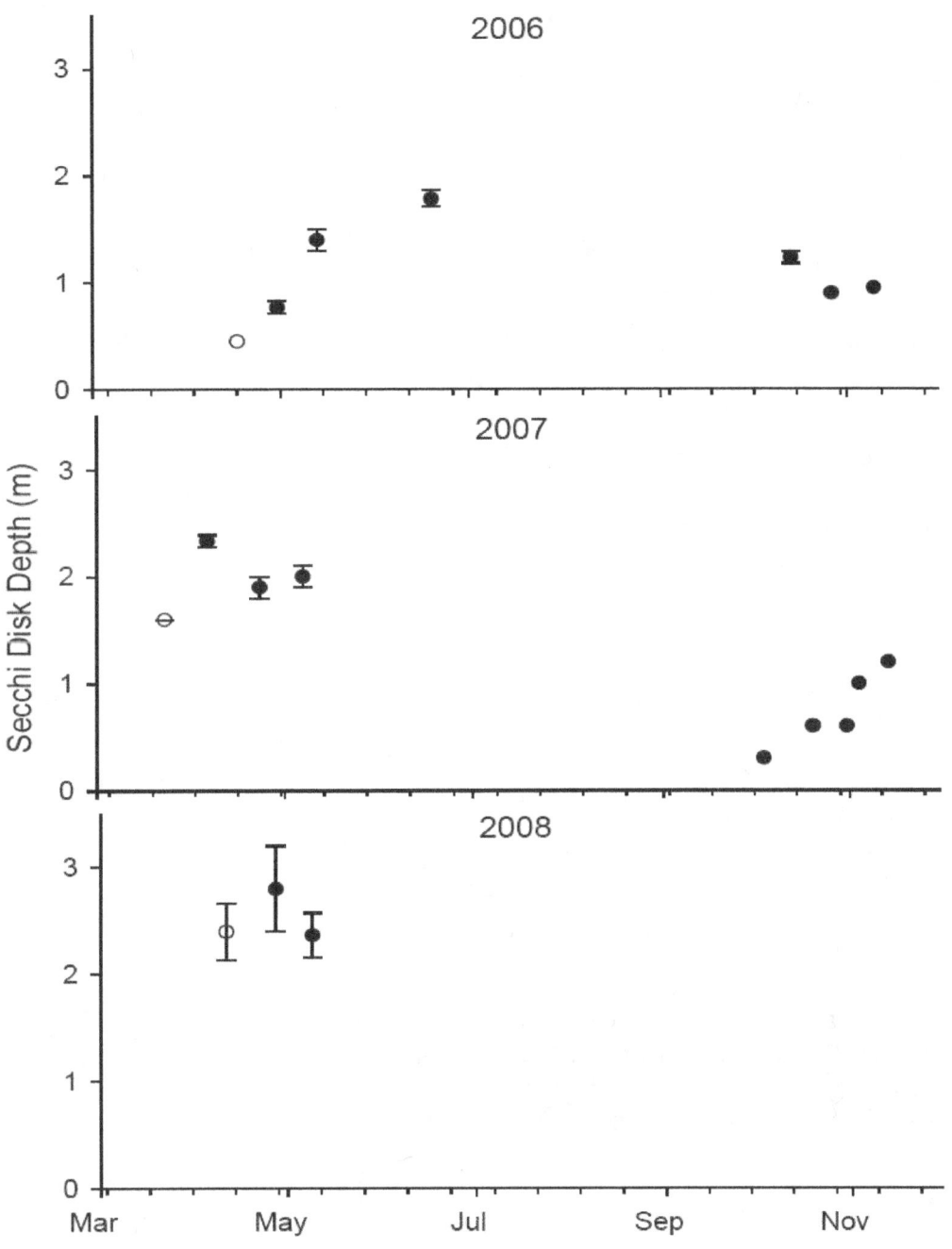

Figure 7. Mean (± SD) Secchi disk depths measured in Beulah Reservoir, 2006–08. Means were derived from sampling at three sites (when water depths permitted).

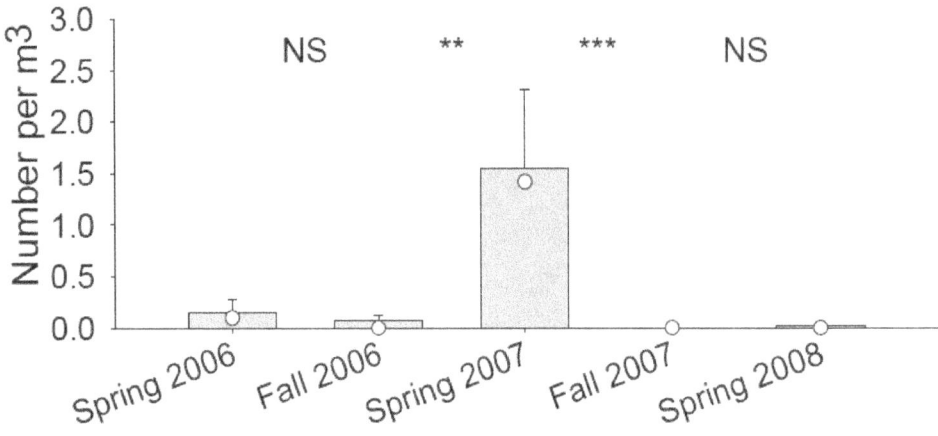

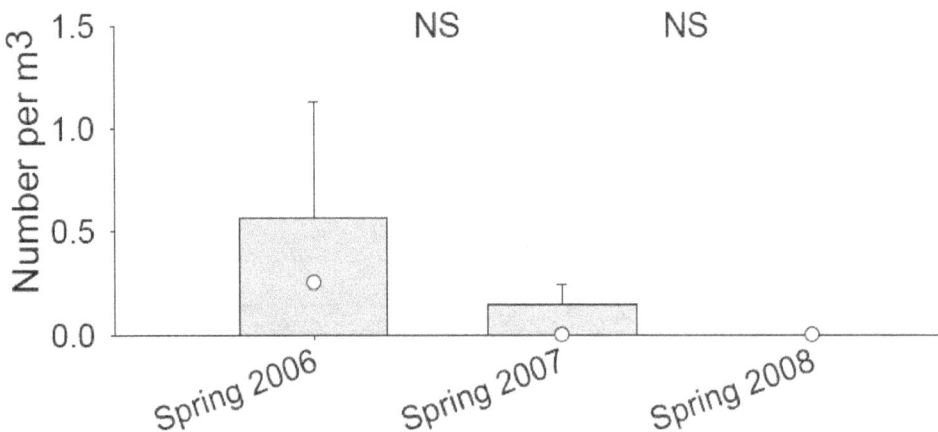

Figure 8. Mean (± 95-percent confidence intervals) and median (white circles) catch per m³ of Hydracarina (upper panel) and chironomids (lower panel) collected with vertical net tows in Beulah Reservoir during spring, 2006–08. Asterisks denote significant differences in catch rates between consecutive sampling periods (that is, * = P < 0.05, ** = P < 0.01, *** = P < 0.001). NS = not significant.

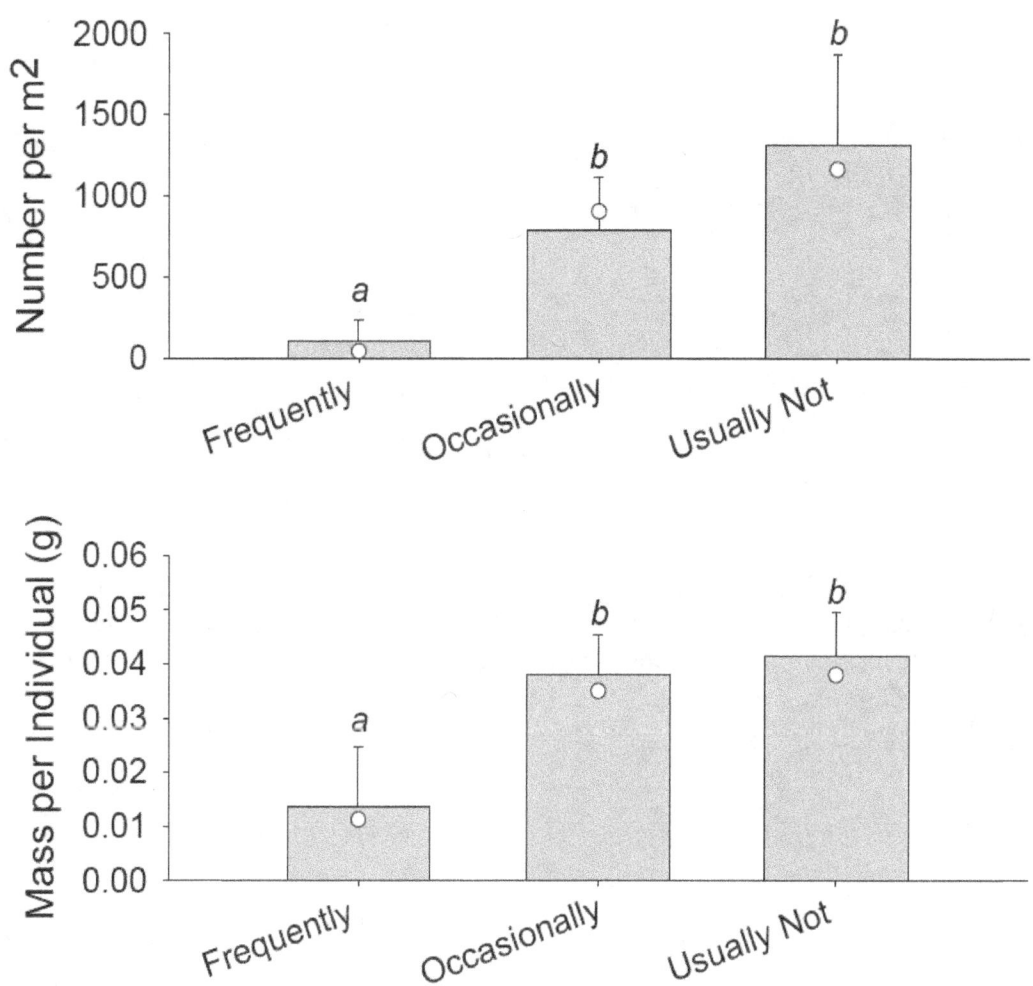

Figure 9. Mean (± 95-percent confidence intervals) and median (white circles) catch per m2 (upper panel) and mass (lower panel) of benthic dipterans collected from locations in Beulah Reservoir that were frequently, occasionally, or usually not dewatered during typical summer drawdown, 2006–07. Means with letters in common did not differ significantly ($P > 0.05$).

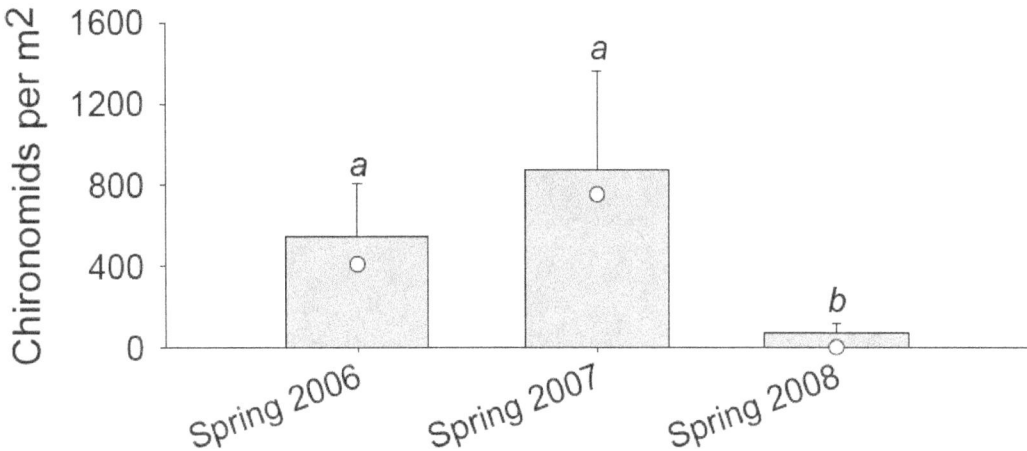

Figure 10. Mean (± 95-percent confidence intervals) and median (white circles) catch per m² of benthic dipterans collected during the spring in Beulah Reservoir, 2006–07. Areas of reservoir substrate that were frequently, occasionally, or usually not dewatered were pooled for analysis. Means with letters in common did not differ significantly (*P* > 0.05).

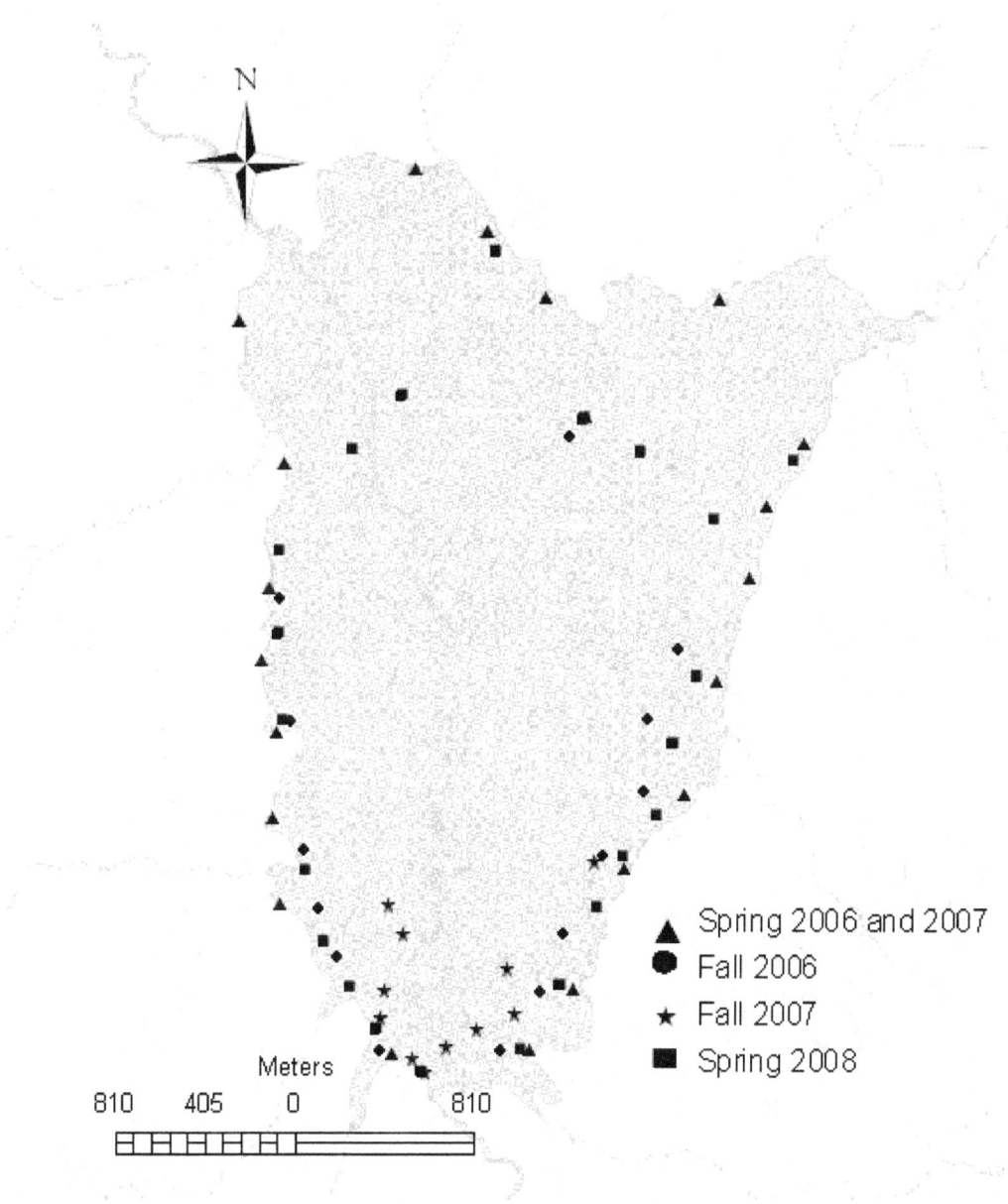

Figure 11. Locations of sampling with fyke nets in Beulah Reservoir, 2006–08.

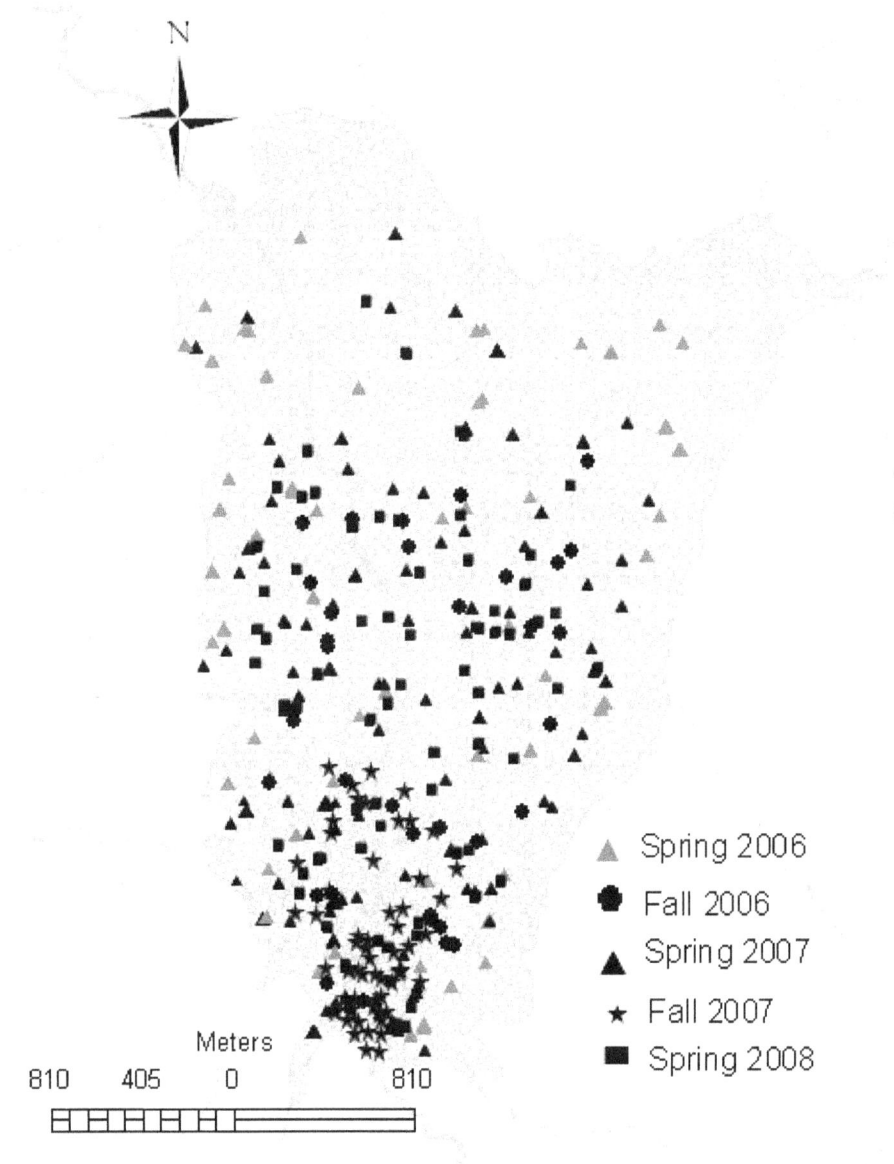

Figure 12. Locations of sampling with gillnets in Beulah Reservoir, 2006–08.

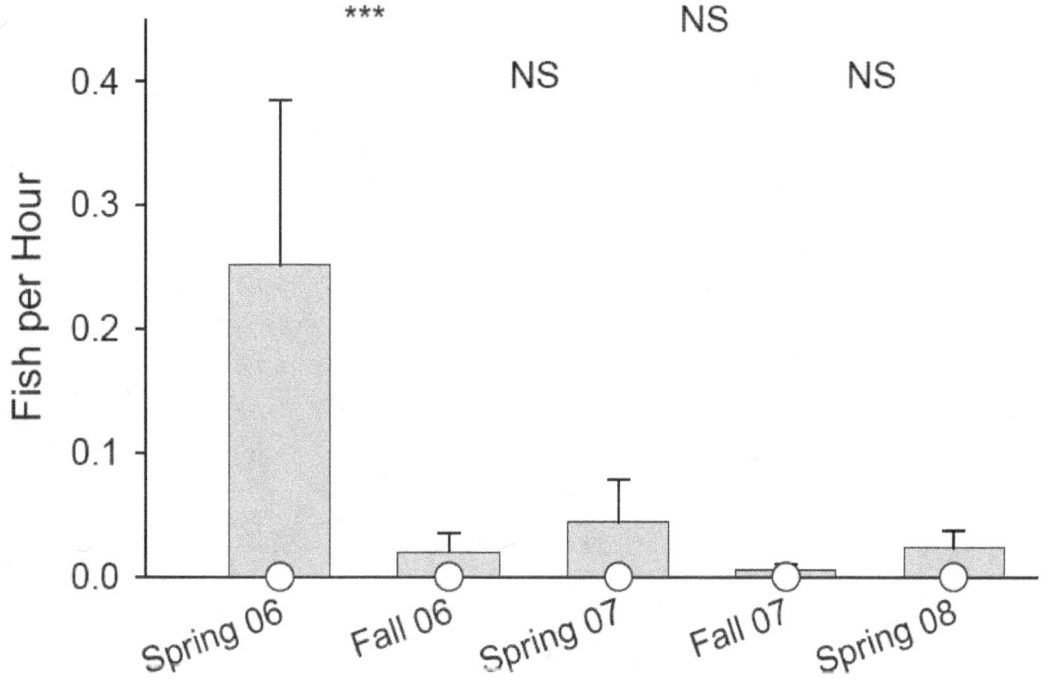

Figure 13. Mean (and 95-percent confidence interval) and median (white circles) catch per hour of fyke nets for species of dace in Beulah Reservoir, 2006–08. Asterisks denote significant differences in catch rates between consecutive sampling periods (that is, * = $P < 0.05$, ** = $P < 0.01$, *** = $P < 0.001$). NS = not significant.

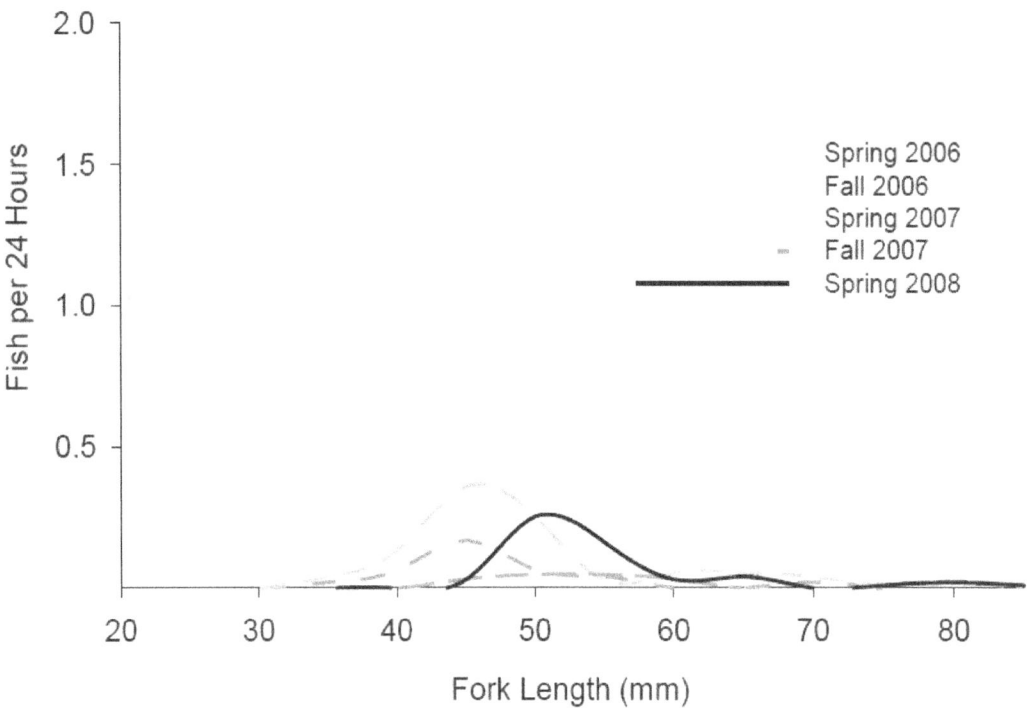

Figure 14. Catch rates of fyke nets for longnose and speckled dace of different sizes in Beulah Reservoir, 2006–08. Data were plotted at 5-mm intervals.

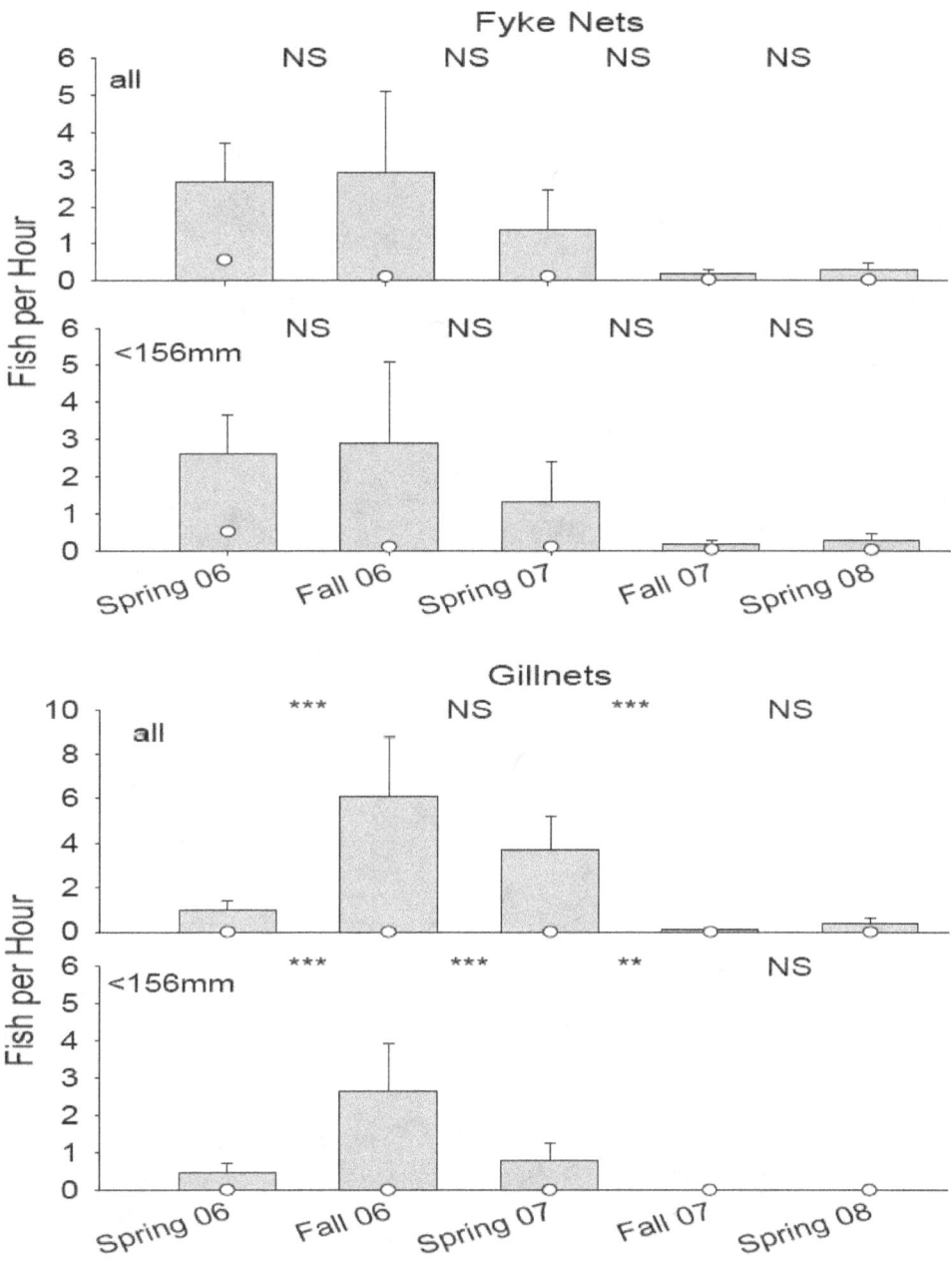

Figure 15. Mean (and 95-percent confidence interval) and median (white circles) catch per hour of fyke nets and gillnets for northern pikeminnow in Beulah Reservoir, 2006–08. Asterisks denote significant differences in catch rates between consecutive sampling periods (that is, * = *P* < 0.05, ** = *P* < 0.01, *** = *P*<0.001). NS = not significant.

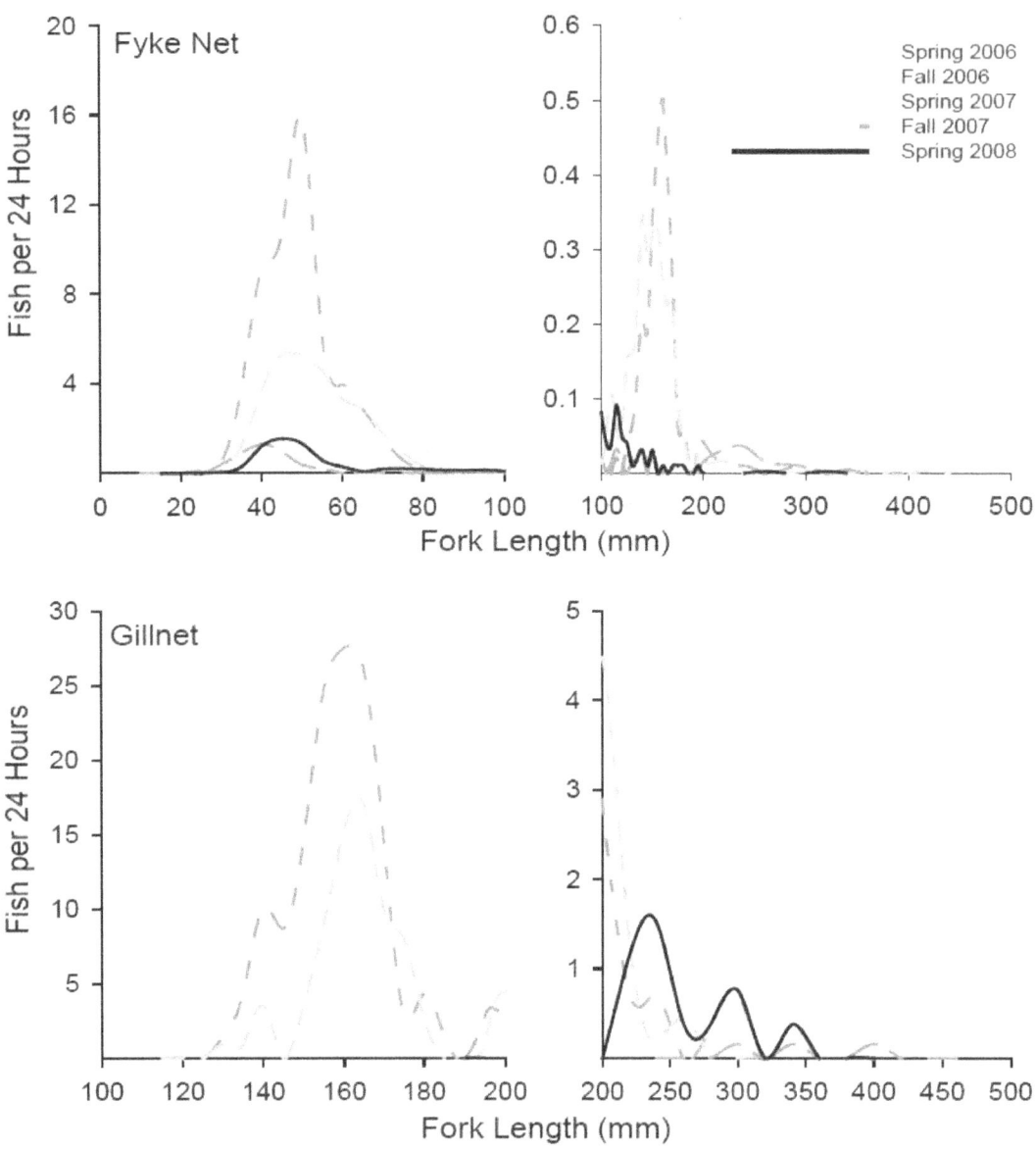

Figure 16. Catch rates of fyke nets (upper panels) and gillnets (lower panels) for northern pikeminnow of different sizes in Beulah Reservoir, 2006–08. Data were plotted at 5-mm intervals for fish <201 mm and at 20-mm intervals for fish >200 mm. Data for larger fish were multiplied by 0.25 to facilitate visual comparisons across sizes.

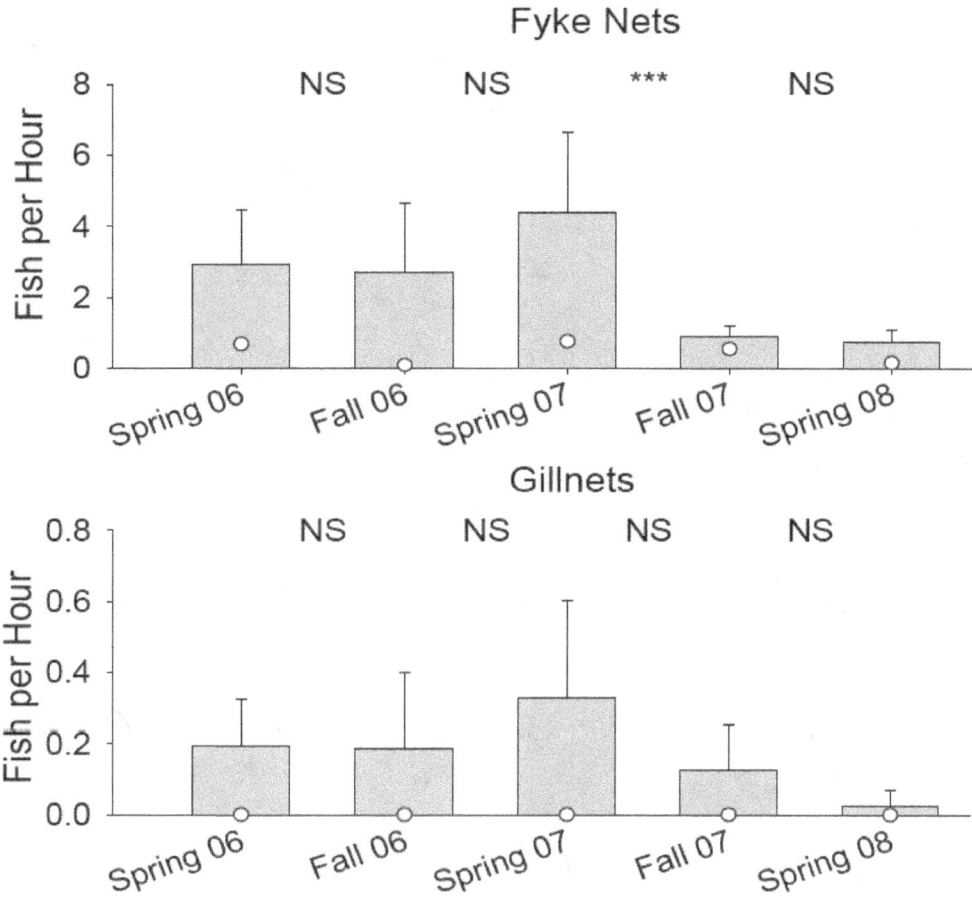

Figure 17. Mean (and 95-percent confidence interval) and median (white circles) catch per hour of fyke nets and gillnets for redside shiners in Beulah Reservoir, 2006–08. Asterisks denote significant differences in catch rates between consecutive sampling periods (that is, * = P < 0.05, ** = P < 0.01, *** = P < 0.001). NS = not significant.

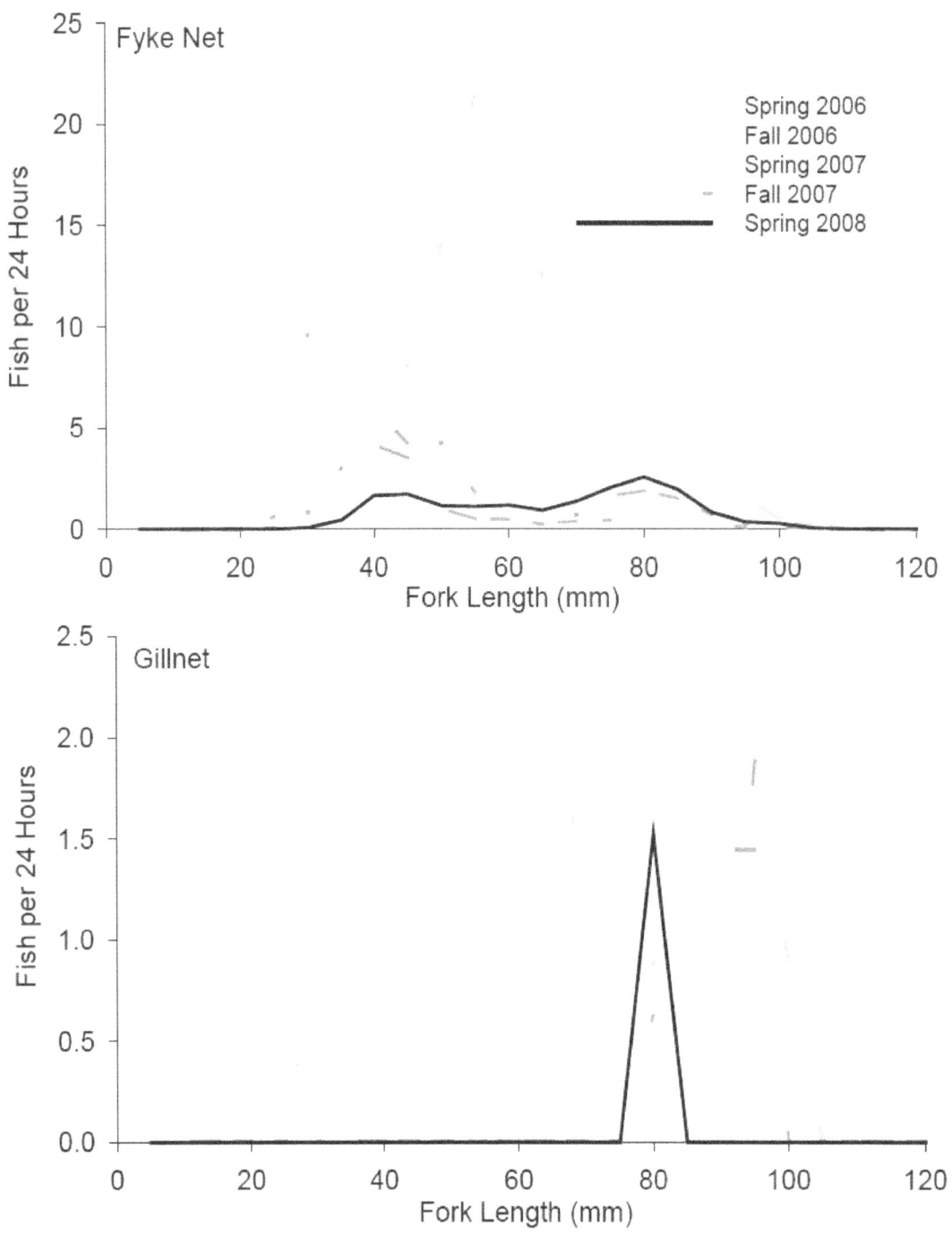

Figure 18. Catch rates of fyke nets (upper panel) and gillnets (lower panel) for redside shiners of different sizes in Beulah Reservoir, 2006–08. Data were plotted at 5-mm intervals.

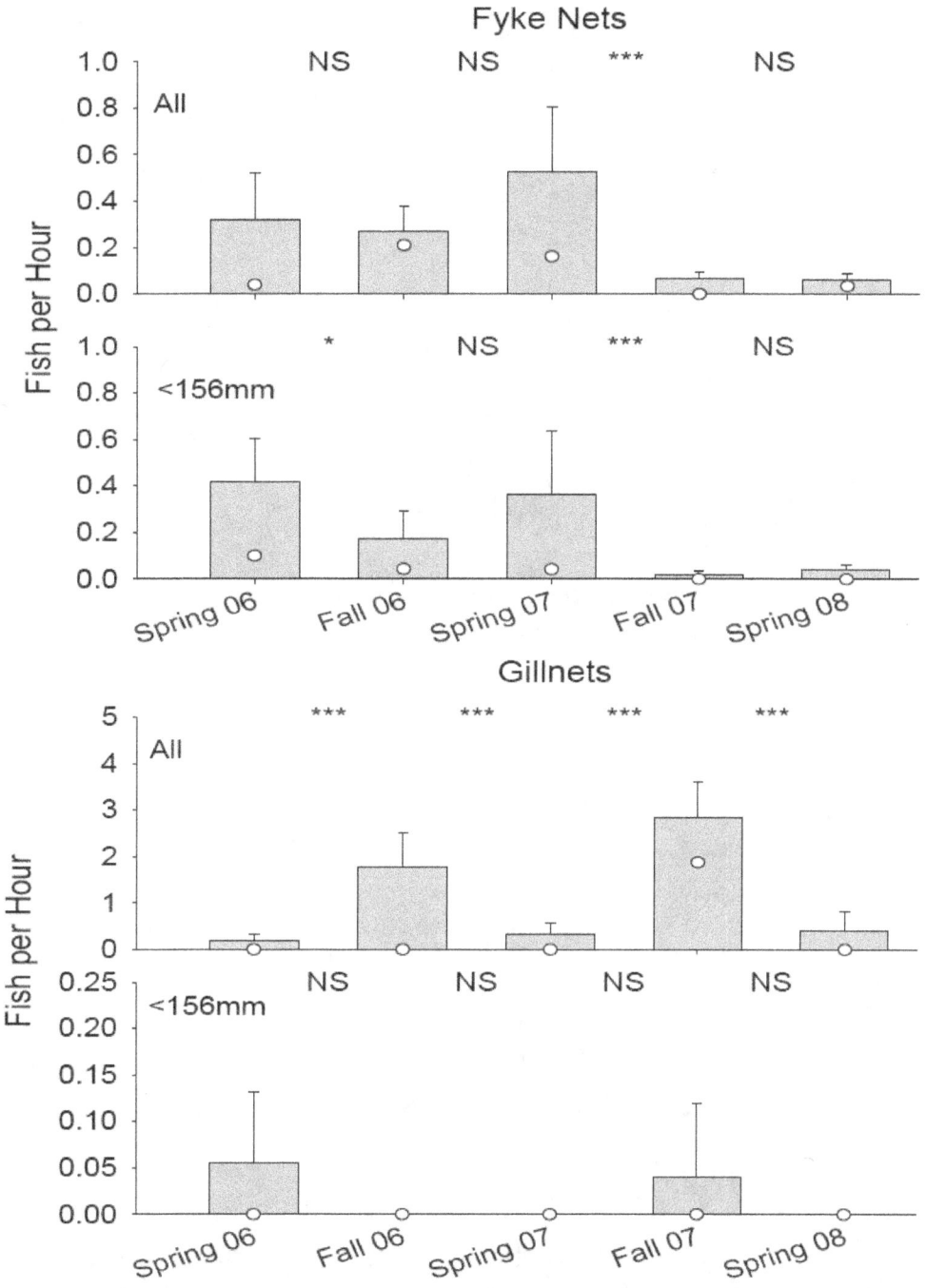

Figure 19. Mean (and 95-percent confidence interval) and median (white circles) catch per hour of fyke nets and gillnets for species of suckers in Beulah Reservoir, 2006–08. Asterisks denote significant differences in catch rates between consecutive sampling periods (that is, * = $P < 0.05$, ** = $P < 0.01$, *** = $P < 0.001$). NS = not significant.

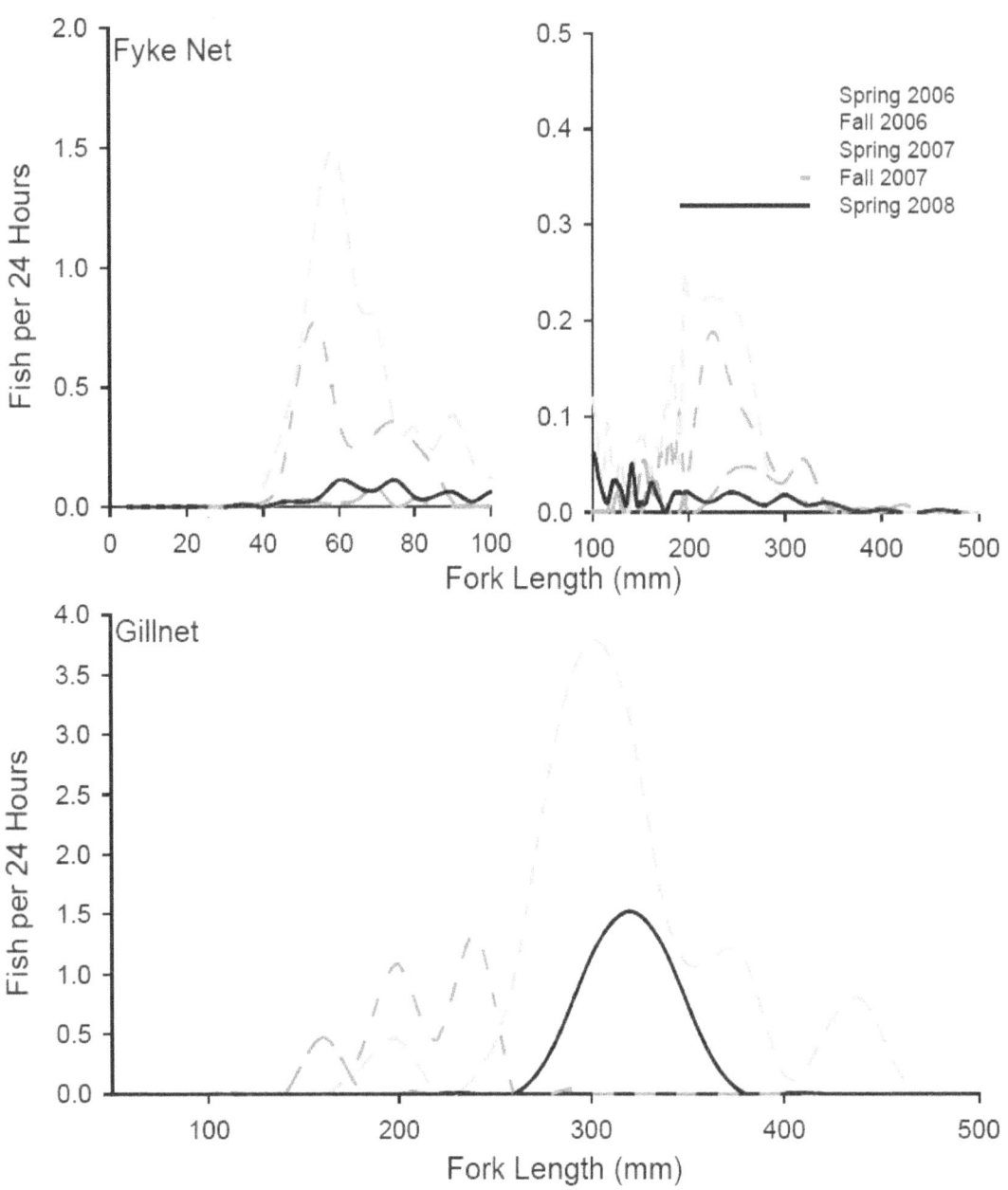

Figure 20. Catch rates of fyke nets (upper panels) and gillnets (lower panel) for bridgelip and largescale suckers of different sizes in Beulah Reservoir, 2006–08. Data were plotted at 5-mm intervals for fish <201 mm and at 20-mm intervals for fish >200 mm. Data plotted for larger fish were multiplied by 0.25 to facilitate comparisons across sizes.

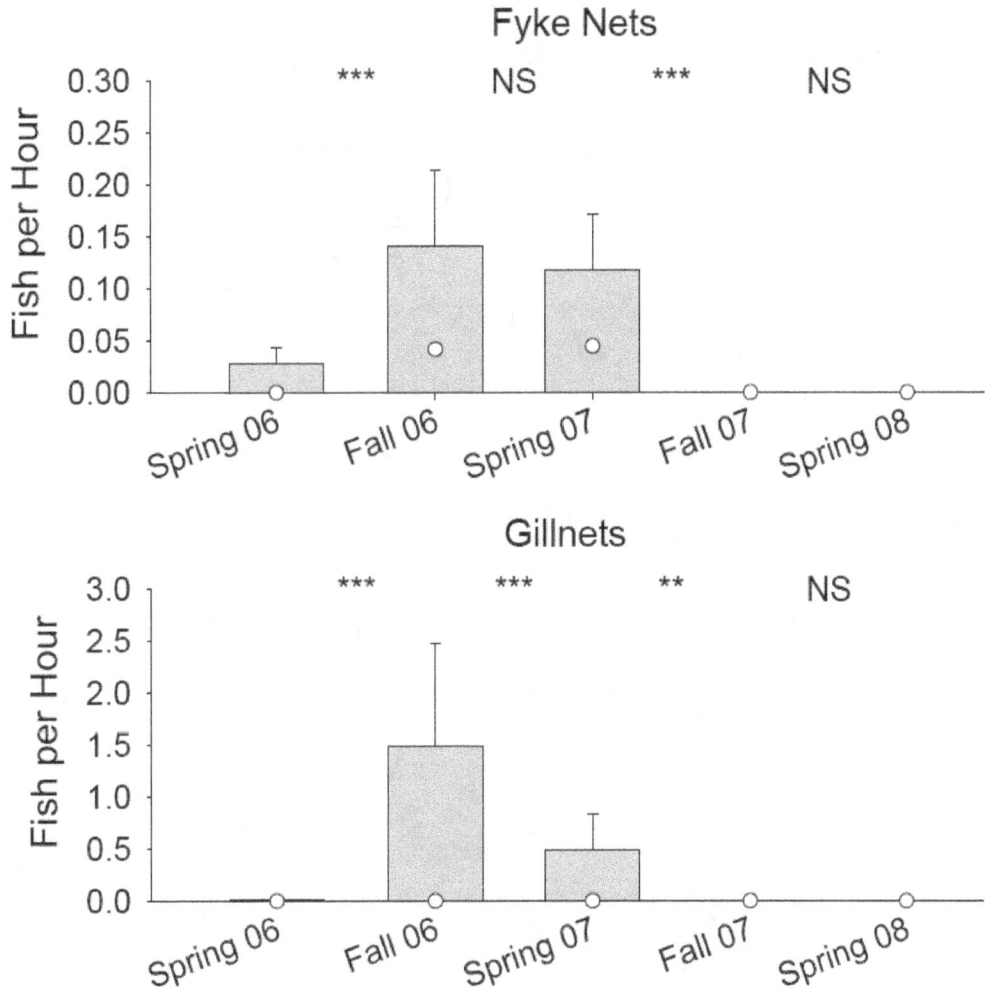

Figure 21. Mean (and 95-percent confidence interval) and median (white circles) catch per hour of fyke nets and gillnets for white crappies in Beulah Reservoir, 2006–08. Asterisks denote significant differences in catch rates between consecutive sampling periods (that is, * = $P < 0.05$, ** = $P < 0.01$, *** = $P < 0.001$). NS = not significant.

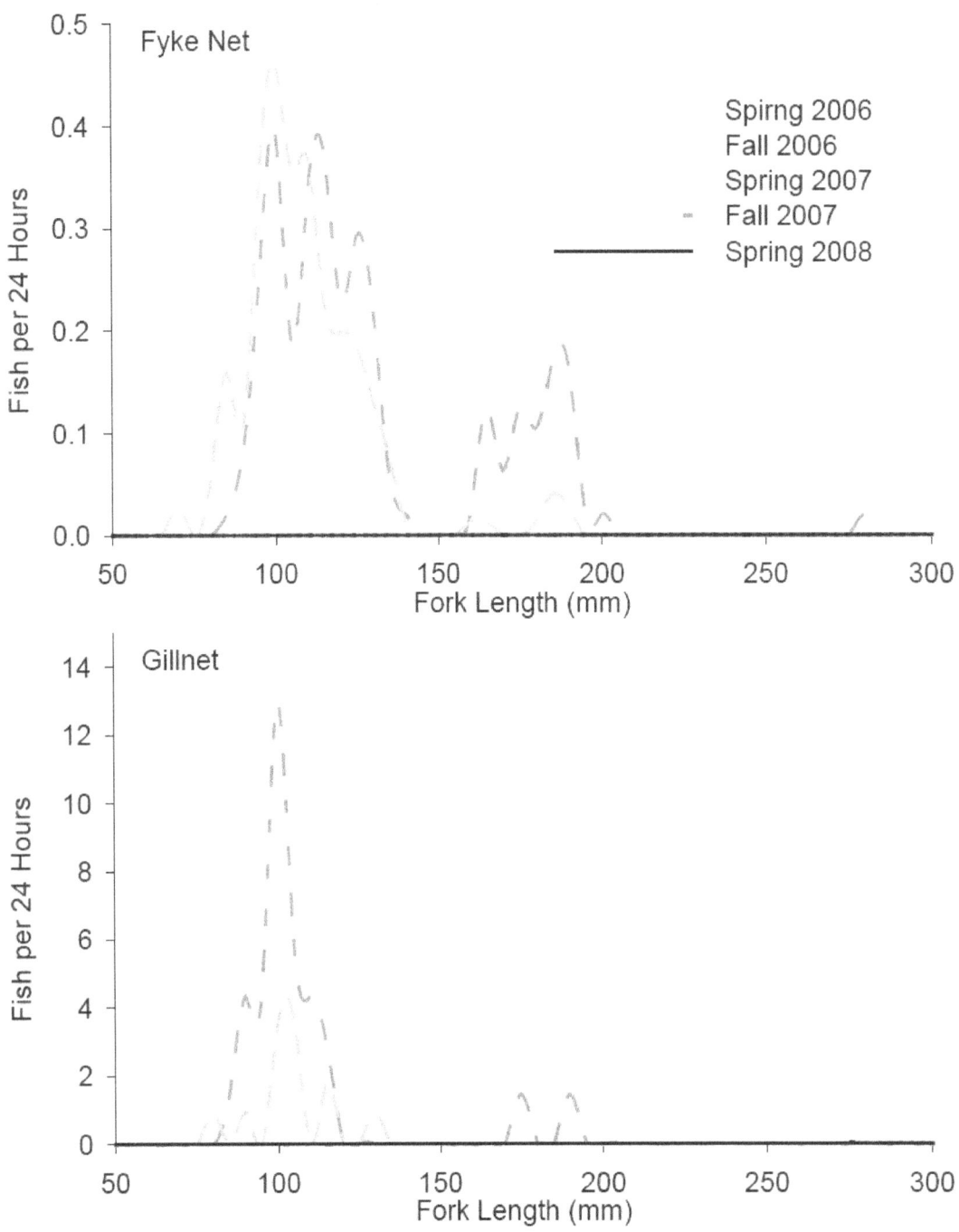

Figure 22. Catch rates of fyke nets (upper panel) and gillnets (lower panel) for white crappies of different sizes in Beulah Reservoir, 2006–08. Data were plotted at 5-mm intervals.

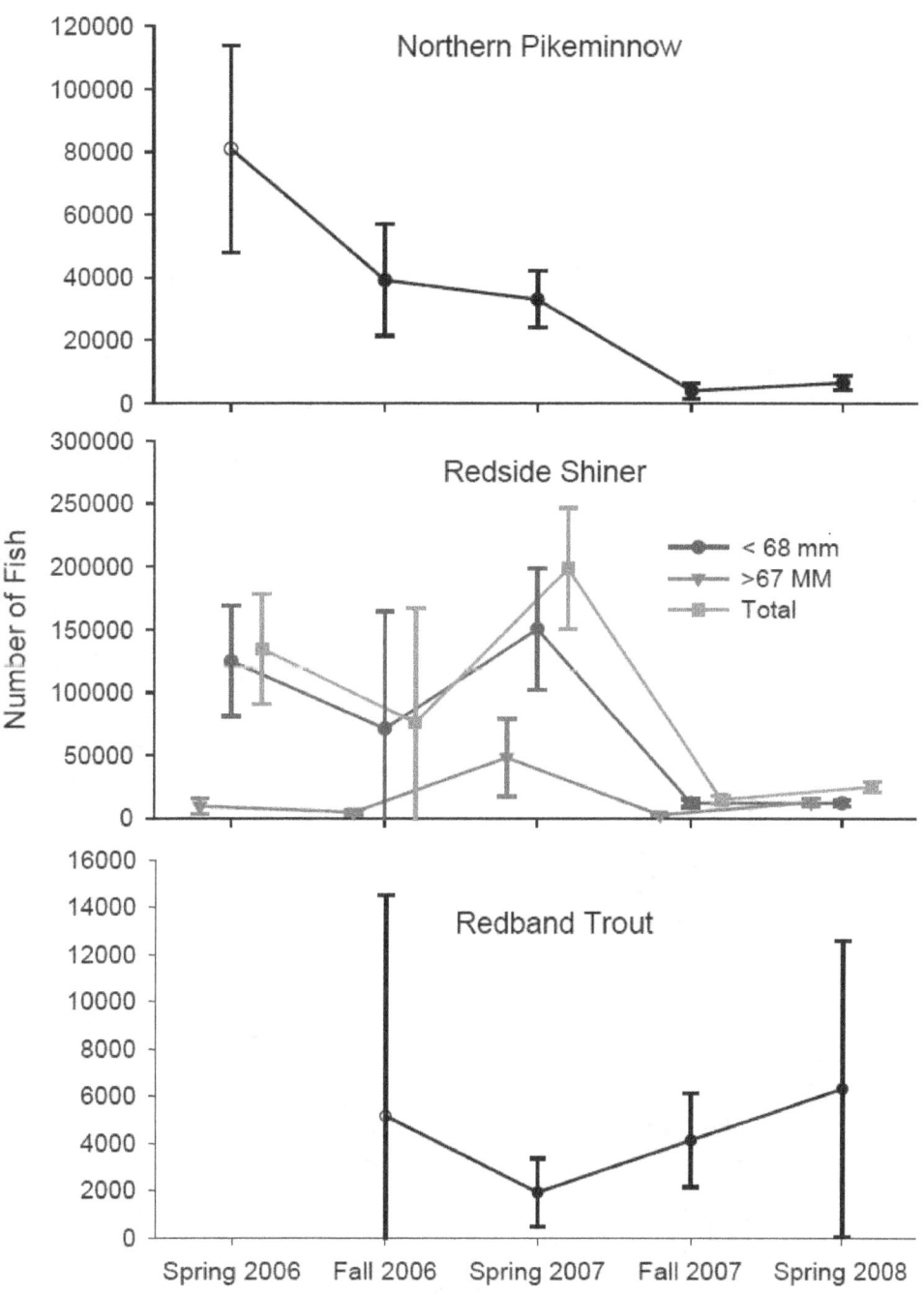

Figure 23. Population abundance estimates (± 95-percent confidence intervals) for northern pikeminnow <156 mm, and redside shiners and redband trout of different sizes in Beulah Reservoir, 2006–08. No data were available for redband trout in the spring of 2006.

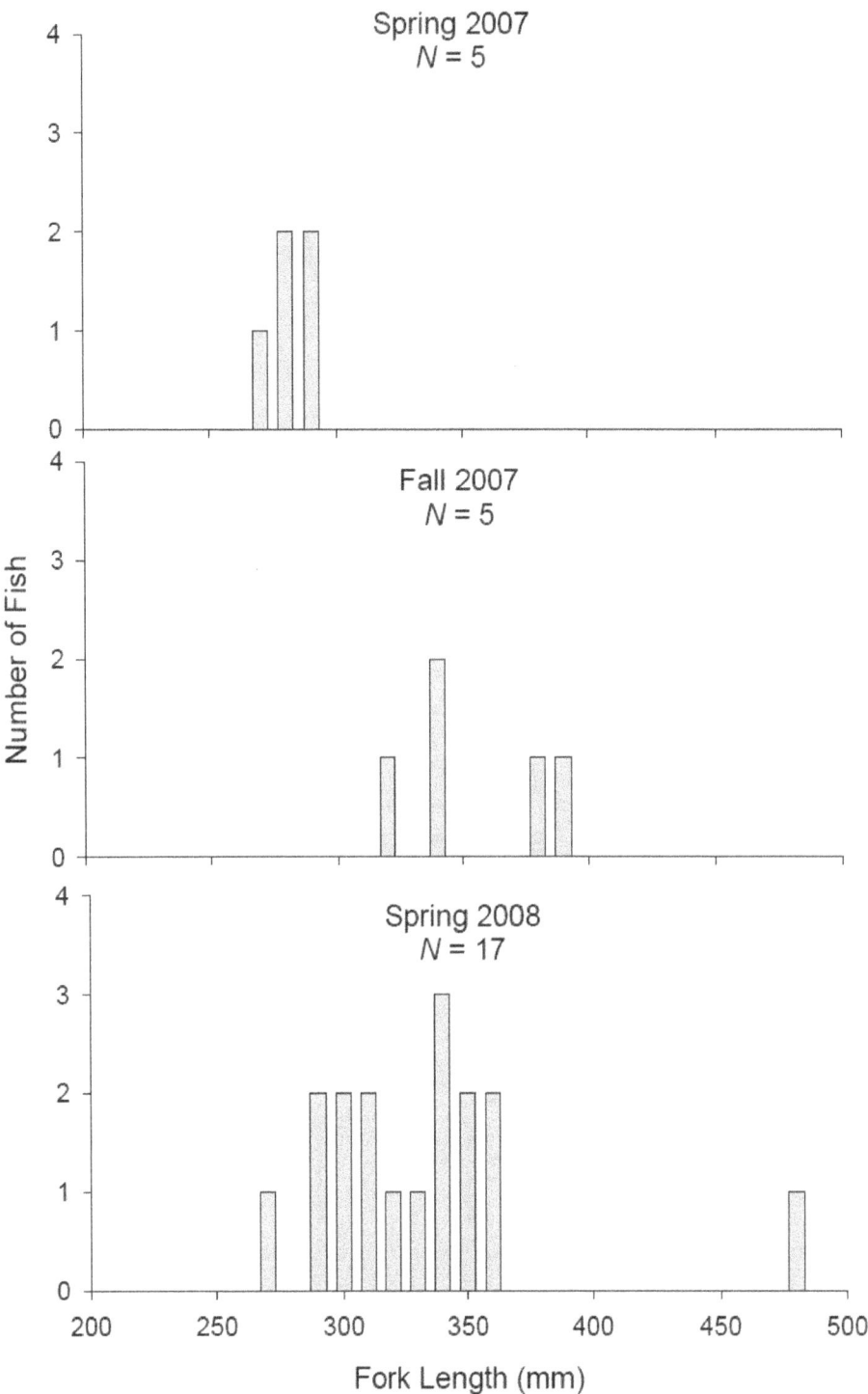

Figure 24. Length-frequency distributions of bull trout collected from Beulah Reservoir, 2007–08.

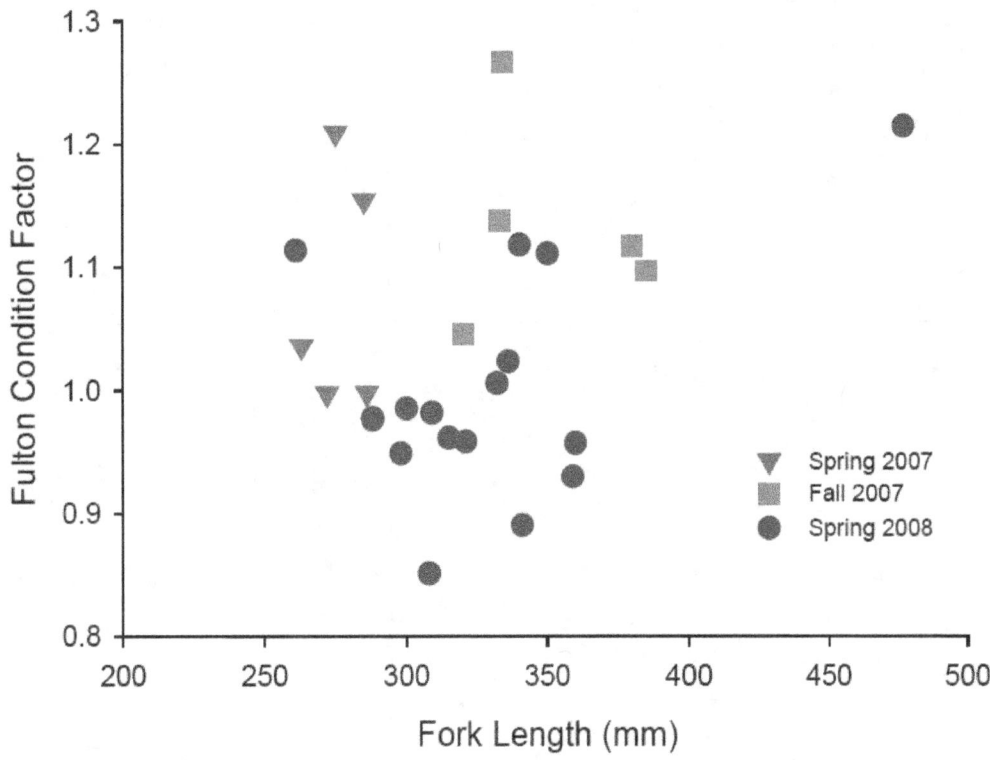

Figure 25. Fulton's condition factor of bull trout collected from Beulah Reservoir, 2007–08.

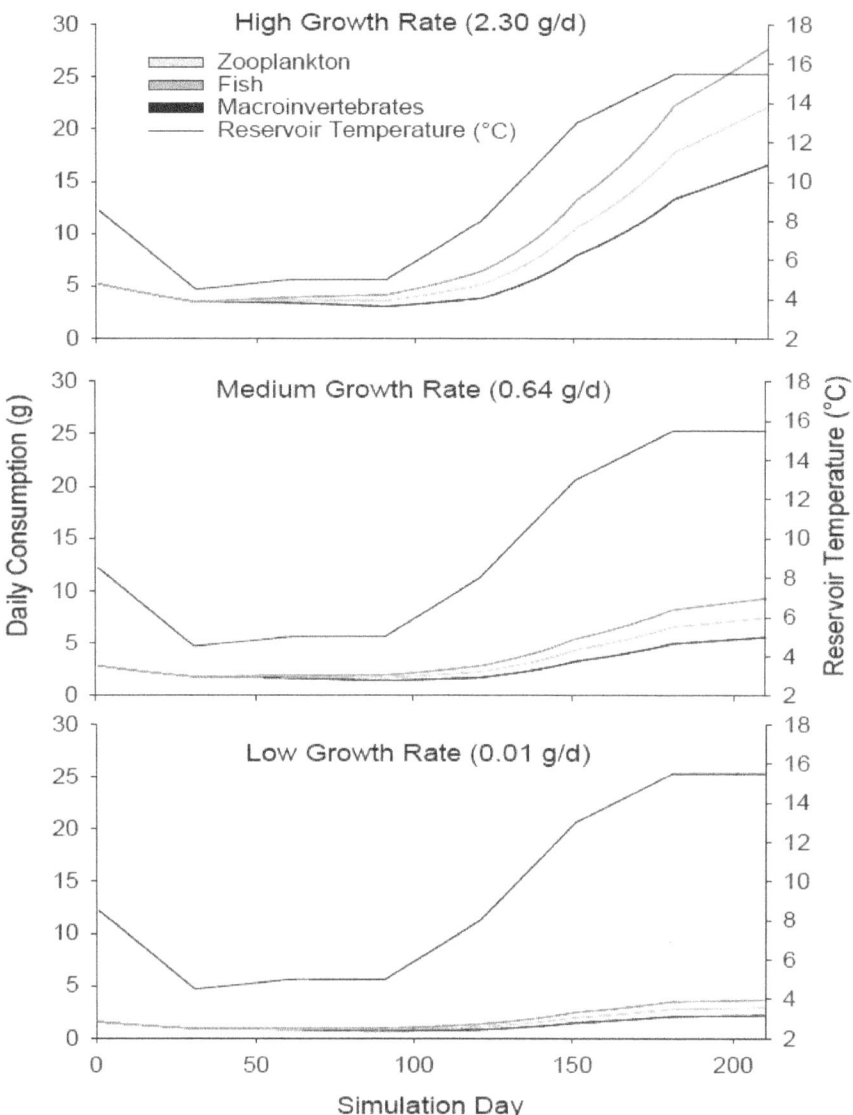

Figure 26. Per capita daily consumption estimates of bull trout for three prey types in Beulah Reservoir under three different growth rates and assuming a diet comprised of 20 percent zooplankton, 60 percent fish, 20 percent invertebrates. Bioenergetics model simulations ran for 210 days from fall through spring. Growth rates of bull trout were representative of fish in Lake Billy Chinook, Oregon (upper panel), Beulah Reservoir and North Fork of the Malheur River (middle panel), and a maintenance growth rate of about 1 percent during the simulation period (lower panel). The solid line denotes the mean daily water temperature in Beulah Reservoir during the simulation period.

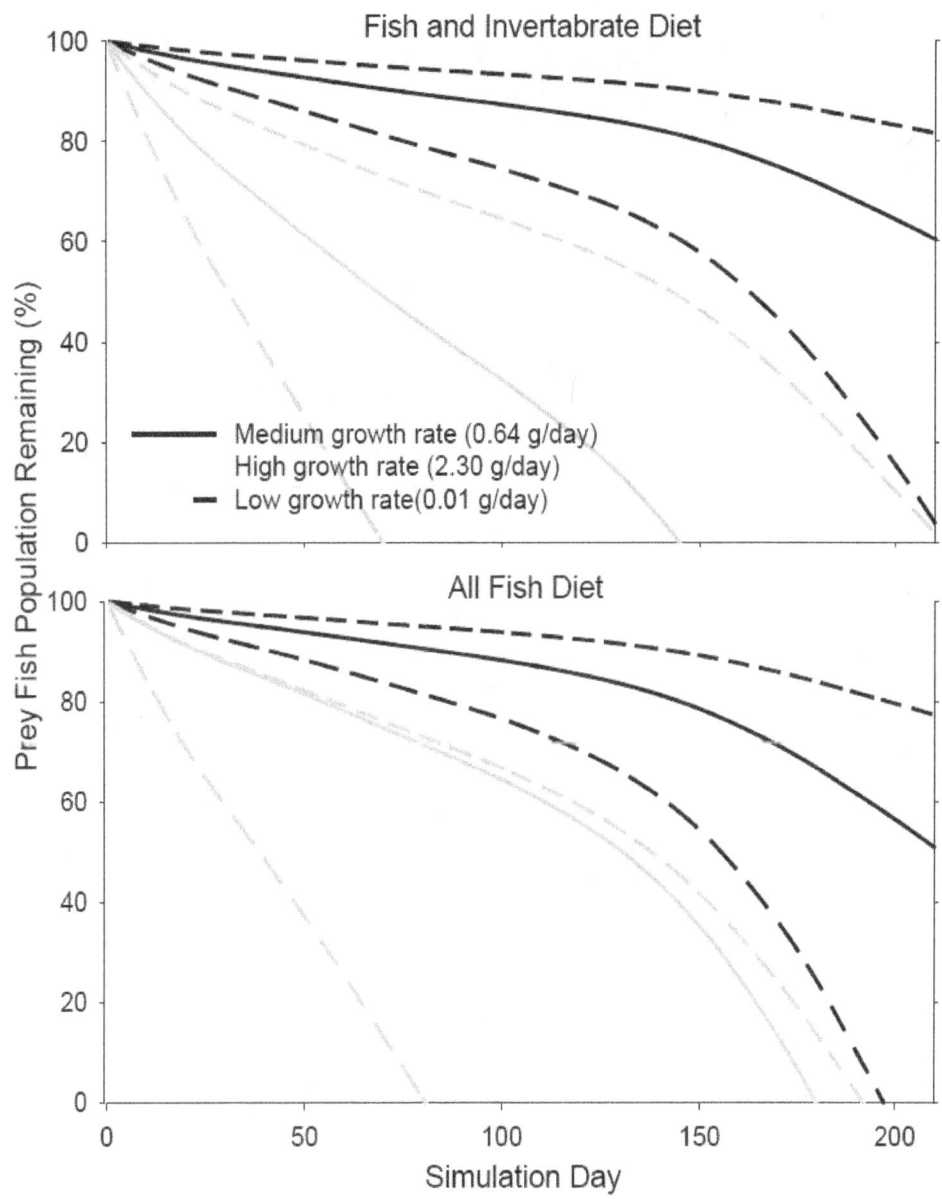

Figure 27. Predicted biomass of fish <156 mm remaining in Beulah Reservoir after consumption by hypothetical populations of 188 (black lines) or 1,000 (grey lines) bull trout with three different growth rates during a 210-day period from fall through spring, 2006–07. Prey fish biomass remaining was calculated by subtracting the cumulative consumption estimates of each population from the initial prey fish biomass in the fall. The simulations in the top graph assumed a diet comprised of 60 percent fish, 20 percent invertebrates, and 20 percent zooplankton, and the bottom graph assumed a diet comprised of only fish.

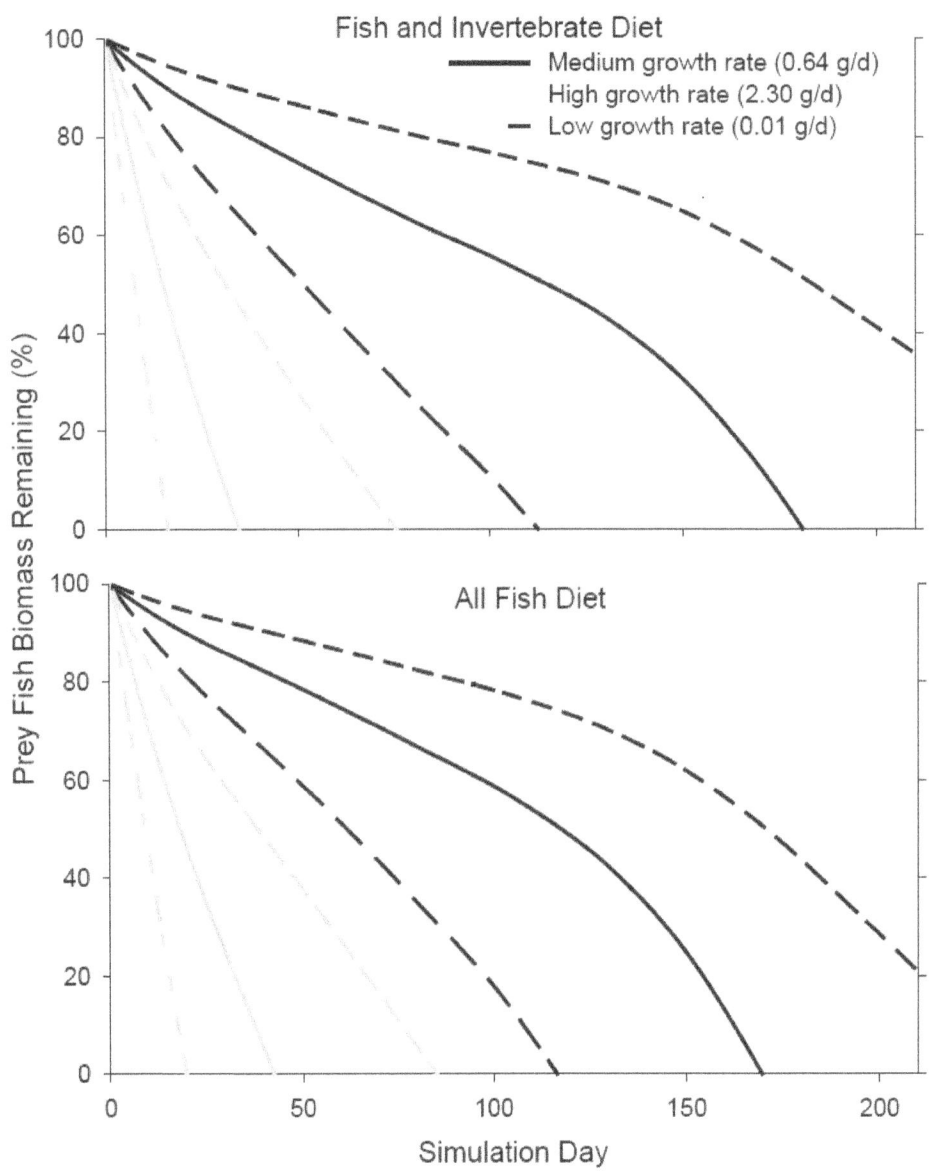

Figure 28. Predicted biomass of fish <156 mm remaining in Beulah Reservoir after consumption by a hypothetical population of 188 (black lines) or 1,000 (grey lines) bull trout with three different growth rates during a 210-day period from fall through spring, 2007–08. Prey fish biomass remaining was calculated by subtracting the cumulative consumption estimates of each population from the initial prey fish biomass in the fall. The simulations in the top graph assumed a diet comprised of 60 percent fish, 20 percent invertebrates, and 20 percent zooplankton, and the bottom graph assumed a diet comprised of only fish.

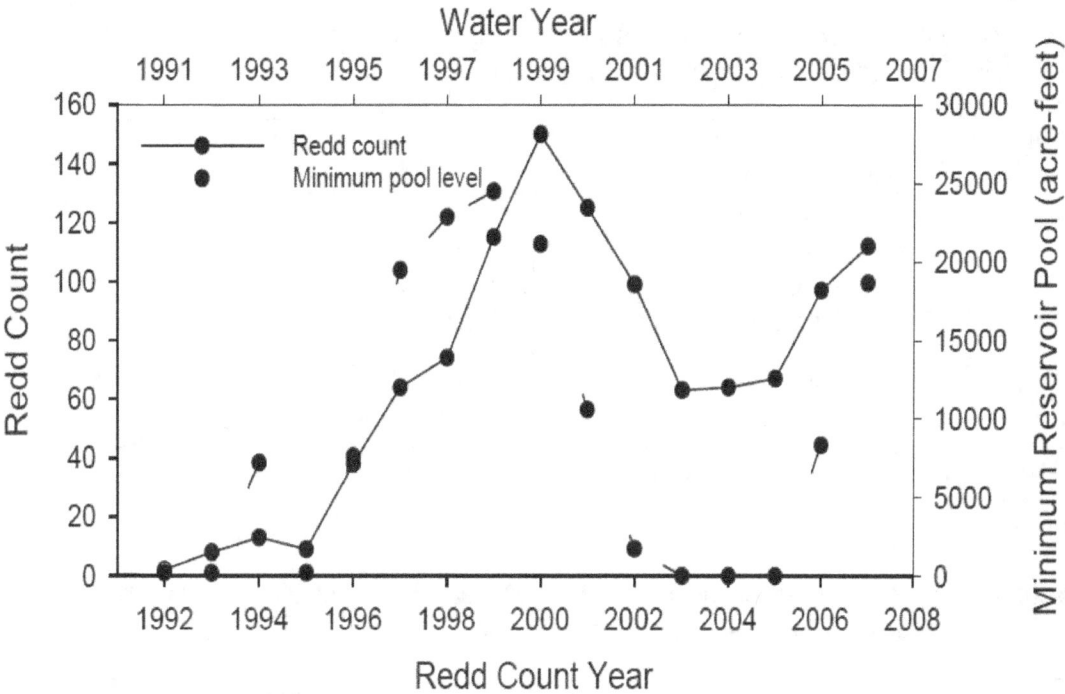

Figure 29. Number of bull trout redds counted in the North Fork Malheur River and the minimum pool level of Beulah Reservoir. The x- axes are plotted offset by 1 year.

Table 1. Day of simulation, reference month, temperature range in Beulah Reservoir during that month, and temperatures used in bioenergetics modeling of bull trout feeding and growth.

Simulation day	Reference month	Temperature range °C	Temperature modeled
1	November	8.5-5.7	8.5
31	December	4.5-4.5	4.5
61	January	5.0-2.0	5.0
91	February	5.0-4.5	5.0
121	March	8.0-6.0	8.0
151	April	13.0-12.5	13.0
181	May	15.5-8.5	15.5

Table 2. Percent occurrence (%O), percent of total number (%N), and percent of total mass (%M) of prey items consumed by bull trout in Beulah Reservoir during the spring (N=5) and fall (N=5) of 2007.

Prey type	Spring 2007			Fall 2007		
	%O	%N	%M	%O	%N	%M
Northern pikeminnow	20	<1	59	0	0	0
Redband trout	20	<1	25	60	30	88
Redside shiner	20	<1	12	60	70	12
Zooplankton	40	95	1	0	0	0
Diptera	20	3	4	0	0	0

Table 3. Mean length (and SD), weight, sample size, and energy density of fish from Beulah Reservoir that we used in bioenergetics modeling of bull trout feeding and growth.

[Fish were collected during the spring and fall of 2006. The energy densities of invertebrates were from the literature and assumed constant between seasons. RBT = redband trout, RSS = redside shiner, NPM = northern pikeminnow]

Season and Species	Mean length (mm)	Mean weight (g)	N	Mean caloric density (kJ/g)
Spring				
RBT	108 (9.3)	14.7 (3.8)	9	5.08 (0.46)
RSS	78 (6.1)	6.8 (1.4)	10	5.63 (0.45)
NPM	99 (18.4)	12.9 (10.4)	10	5.36 (0.61)
All Fish	94 (18)	11.3 (7.0)	29	5.37 (0.55)
	-	-	-	
Fall				
RBT	88 (9.2)	6.7 (2.2)	9	5.56 (0.24)
RSS	70 (12.7)	4.6 (2.3)	11	5.07 (0.30)
NPM	63 (5.5)	2.7 (0.6)	10	5.47 (0.37)
All Fish	73 (13.9)	4.6 (2.4)	30	5.35 (0.37)
Daphnia	-	-	-	3.56
Invertebrates	-	-	-	3.35

Table 4. Fyke net and gillnet sampling effort and overall catch rates of fish in Beulah Reservoir, 2006–08.

	Fyke net				Gillnet			
Sampling period	N of sets	Hours sampled	Mean soak time (h)	Overall catch (fish/hour)	N of sets	Hours sampled	Mean soak time (h)	Overall catch (fish/hour)
Spring 2006	71	1,650	23	6.0	142	61.3	0.4	1.8
Fall 2006	39	1,143	29	5.0	47	16.6	0.4	10.6
Spring 2007	76	1,813	24	6.5	73	27.2	0.4	4.7
Fall 2007	65	1,514	23	1.5	83	38.2	0.5	4.5
Spring 2008	100	2,378	24	1.2	80	36.5	0.5	1.8

Table 5. Bioenergetics model estimates of consumption (kg) by bull trout with a hypothetical population size of 188 or 1,000 fish using three growth rates and two diet scenarios.

[Simulations ran for 210 days during late fall through spring]

Growth rate and population size	Fish and invertebrate diet			All fish Diet
	Fish	Macro-invertebrates	Zoo-plankton	Fish
0.01 g/day				
188	49.1	11.3	11.3	60.5
1,000	261.0	60.0	60.0	321.8
0.64 g/day				
188	105.1	25.4	25.4	130.5
1,000	559.2	135.2	135.2	694.4
2.30 g/day				
188	255.3	65.9	65.9	319.8
1,000	1,357.9	350.4	350.4	1701.0

Table 6. Number of rainbow trout that were stocked in Beulah Reservoir, 2004–08.

[T = triploid fish]

Year	Date stocked	Number stocked	Fish Stock
2004	5/12/2004	35,000	Oak Springs
2005	5/12/2005	30,000	Oak Springs
2006	5/16/2006	79,974	Oak Springs (T=47%)
2007	5/15/2007	80,000	Oak Springs (T)
2008	5/15/2008	29,970	Oak Springs (T)

www.ingramcontent.com/pod-product-compliance
Lightning Source LLC
Chambersburg PA
CBHW080442290526
45791CB00008BA/2581